MORRIS AUTOMATED INFORMATION NETWORK

0 1022 0385956 0

D1518916

DISCARDED

The Morristown & Morris Township Library
One Miller Rd.
Morristown, NJ 07960

DISCARDED

COMPACT *Research*

Gay Rights

Peggy J. Parks

Current Issues

ReferencePoint
Press™

San Diego, CA

© 2009 ReferencePoint Press, Inc.

For more information, contact:
ReferencePoint Press, Inc.
PO Box 27779
San Diego, CA 92198
www. ReferencePointPress.com

ALL RIGHTS RESERVED.
No part of this work covered by the copyright hereon may be reproduced or used in any form or by any means—graphic, electronic, or mechanical, including photocopying, recording, taping, Web distribution, or information storage retrieval systems—without the written permission of the publisher.

Picture credits:
Maury Aaseng: 32–35, 49–52, 66–69, 82–84
AP Images: 13,16

LIBRARY OF CONGRESS CATALOGING-IN-PUBLICATION DATA

Parks, Peggy J., 1951–
 Gay rights / by Peggy J. Parks.
  p. cm. — (Compact research series)
 Includes bibliographical references and index.
 ISBN-13: 978-1-60152-063-0 (hardback)
 ISBN-10: 1-60152-063-8 (hardback)
 1. Gay rights—United States. 2. Gays—Legal status, laws, etc.—United States. I. Title.
 HQ76.8.U5P37 2008
 323.3'2940973—dc22

                                                           2008031595

Contents

Foreword

> **❝ Where is the knowledge we have lost in information? ❞**

—T.S. Eliot, "The Rock."

As modern civilization continues to evolve, its ability to create, store, distribute, and access information expands exponentially. The explosion of information from all media continues to increase at a phenomenal rate. By 2020 some experts predict the worldwide information base will double every 73 days. While access to diverse sources of information and perspectives is paramount to any democratic society, information alone cannot help people gain knowledge and understanding. Information must be organized and presented clearly and succinctly in order to be understood. The challenge in the digital age becomes not the creation of information, but how best to sort, organize, enhance, and present information.

ReferencePoint Press developed the *Compact Research* series with this challenge of the information age in mind. More than any other subject area today, researching current issues can yield vast, diverse, and unqualified information that can be intimidating and overwhelming for even the most advanced and motivated researcher. The *Compact Research* series offers a compact, relevant, intelligent, and conveniently organized collection of information covering a variety of current topics ranging from illegal immigration and methamphetamine to diseases such as anorexia and meningitis.

The series focuses on three types of information: objective single-author narratives, opinion-based primary source quotations, and facts and statistics. The clearly written objective narratives provide context and reliable background information. Primary source quotes are carefully selected and cited, exposing the reader to differing points of view. And facts and statistics sections aid the reader in evaluating perspectives. Presenting these key types of information creates a richer, more balanced learning experience.

For better understanding and convenience, the series enhances information by organizing it into narrower topics and adding design features that make it easy for a reader to identify desired content. For example, in *Compact Research: Illegal Immigration*, a chapter covering the economic impact of illegal immigration has an objective narrative explaining the various ways the economy is impacted, a balanced section of numerous primary source quotes on the topic, followed by facts and full-color illustrations to encourage evaluation of contrasting perspectives.

The ancient Roman philosopher Lucius Annaeus Seneca wrote, "It is quality rather than quantity that matters." More than just a collection of content, the *Compact Research* series is simply committed to creating, finding, organizing, and presenting the most relevant and appropriate amount of information on a current topic in a user-friendly style that invites, intrigues, and fosters understanding.

Gay Rights at a Glance

Launch of the Gay Rights Movement

In June 1969 a massive riot broke out in New York City and ushered in the gay rights movement. The uprising, which came to be known as the Stonewall Riots, led to the formation of the Gay Liberation Front and other gay and lesbian advocacy organizations.

Civil Rights

Although gays and lesbians have made progress over the years, there is still no federal law that protects them from discrimination in employment, housing, or public accommodations.

Sodomy Laws

Prior to a ruling by the U.S. Supreme Court in 2003, legislation in many states made sodomy a crime, even if the sexual acts occurred in the privacy of one's own home. In 2003 the U.S. Supreme Court ruled that sodomy laws were unconstitutional.

AIDS Epidemic

In the 1980s the gay rights movement suffered an enormous setback after acquired immunodeficiency syndrome (AIDS) was determined to be spread through anal intercourse.

Gays and Lesbians in the Military

The Don't Ask, Don't Tell policy allows homosexuals to serve in the military as long as they do not tell anyone about their sexual orientation.

Gay and Lesbian Marriage

The Defense of Marriage Act, which was signed into law in 1996, defines marriage as being between one man and one woman and allows states to set their own policies about same-sex marriage.

Adopting Children

Most states allow gays and lesbians to adopt children; Florida is the only state that bans it outright, either by gay or lesbian singles or couples.

Future Goals

The two main priorities of the gay rights movement are to repeal the military's Don't Ask, Don't Tell policy and to achieve the right to legally marry anywhere in the United States.

Overview

Overview

“ Don't any of you wonder why heterosexuals treat gays so brutally year after year after year, as your people take away our manhood, our womanhood, our person-hood? Why, even as we die you don't leave us alone.”

—Larry Kramer, "Why Do Straights Hate Gays?"

“ You know, I hate gay people, so I let it be known. I don't like gay people and I don't like to be around gay people. I am homophobic. I don't like it. It shouldn't be in the world or in the United States.”

—Tim Hardaway, quoted in ESPN, "Retired NBA Star Hardaway Says He Hates 'Gay People.'"

On the evening of June 27, 1969, a massive riot broke out in the Greenwich Village area of New York City. The uproar was sparked by a police raid that occurred at the Stonewall Inn, a bar owned by the mafia that was popular with gay men. Even though such raids were common and patrons rarely protested or resisted arrest, this time they decided they had been harassed enough. As officers prepared to transport a group of them to the police station, violence erupted in the streets. Hundreds of men began fighting back, hurling bricks, stones, and bottles at police while shouting "Gay Power!" The crowd swelled to as many as 2,000 people, and the violence escalated. Even larger crowds returned to continue protesting the next night, and again several nights after that. This backlash, which came to be known as the Stonewall Riots, strength-ened the resolve of the homosexual community to take a stand against discrimination and harassment, and it led to the founding of a protest group in New York City known as the Gay Liberation Front. The gay rights movement had been born, as Columbia University's Ken Harlin writes:

> Prior to that summer there was little public expression of the lives and experiences of gays and lesbians. The Stonewall Riots marked the beginning of the gay liberation movement that has transformed the oppression of gays and lesbians into calls for pride and action. In the past twenty-five years we have all been witness to an astonishing flowering of gay culture that has changed this country and beyond, forever.[1]

In the decades since the Stonewall Riots took place, progress has been made in the fight for gay rights. Yet even today, gay men and lesbians are still not afforded many of the same rights as heterosexuals, and are often ostracized by society. This sort of discrimination is at the very heart of the gay rights movement, which vows to ensure equality for all people, regardless of their sexual orientation.

History of Gay Rights

The gay rights movement was quietly gaining strength many years before the Stonewall Riots broke out. In 1924 a Chicago postal worker named Henry Gerber founded the Society for Human Rights, America's first formally organized homosexual rights group. Gerber had been inspired by the open homosexual culture in his native Germany, and he wanted to help spawn the same sort of acceptance in the United States. His group published two issues of a newsletter entitled *Friendship and Freedom*, the first American publication for gays and lesbians. Within a few months police found out about the organization and raided its headquarters, arresting Gerber and hauling him off to jail. Although he escaped being convicted, he was fired by the post office when his superiors learned what had happened.

> " Hundreds of men began fighting back, hurling bricks, stones, and bottles at police while shouting "Gay Power!" "

The 1950s were a time of growth for the gay rights movement. The Mattachine Society, a secretive network of homosexuals, was founded in Los Angeles 1950 by an American Communist named Harry Hay. A few years later some members formed a spin-off group known as ONE, Incorporated, and they published a bold new magazine called *ONE*. The magazine's stance was that gays and lesbians were an oppressed minority who endured insufferable discrimination and oppression. In 1955 a small group of women founded the Daughters of Bilitis, the first advocacy group for lesbians. Over the following years, the Mattachine Society, ONE, Incorporated, and the Daughters of Bilitis became known as the leading representatives of America's growing gay rights movement.

Sodomy Laws

Throughout history many gay men who were arrested by law enforcement were charged with the crime of sodomy. As recently as the 1970s nearly all states had laws in place that made sodomy illegal for people of the opposite sex as well as those of the same sex. The laws were rarely, if ever, enforced among heterosexual couples, but if two men were caught in the act of sodomy, they could be arrested and severely punished. Virginia's sodomy law was challenged in 1976, and the case was the first of its kind to reach the U.S. Supreme Court. In a complaint entitled *Doe v. Commonwealth Attorney of Virginia*, the state's sodomy law was said to be a violation of the right to privacy. The Court disagreed, however, ruling that the law was constitutional and was to be upheld. Ten years later another sodomy case, *Bowers v. Hardwick*, also reached the Supreme Court. At issue was Georgia's law, which had been in place since 1816 and stated: "A person commits the offense of sodomy when he performs or submits to any sexual act involving the sex organs of one person and the mouth or anus of another. . . . A person convicted of the offense of sodomy shall be punished by imprisonment for not less than one nor more than 20 years."[2] The complaint was filed by Michael Hardwick, an Atlanta bartender who in 1982 was arrested in his own bedroom for having sex with another man. Hardwick contended that the

> " Throughout history many gay men who were arrested by law enforcement were charged with the crime of sodomy. "

arrest was an invasion of privacy and a violation of his constitutional rights. Although the federal court of appeals had ruled in favor of Hardwick, the Supreme Court disagreed and struck the decision down. On June 30, 1986, the Court ruled 5 to 4 that the Georgia law was constitutional, that states had the right to prosecute homosexual relations as a felony, and the fact that the homosexual acts occurred in the privacy of one's home did not matter.

In 2003 the Supreme Court again addressed the issue of sodomy in a case known as *Lawrence et al. v. Texas*. In responding to a weapons disturbance in an apartment, Houston police entered a man's apartment and found him having sex with another man. The officers arrested both men, and they were later convicted of "deviate sexual intercourse in violation of a Texas statute forbidding two persons of the same sex to engage in certain intimate sexual conduct."[3] In its June 2003 ruling the Supreme Court struck down the Texas law, as well as all sodomy laws in the United States, declaring them to be unconstitutional. This was considered to be a major victory for the gay rights movement, as federal law dictated that gay men could no longer be punished for what went on in the privacy of their own homes.

Are Gay Rights Protected in the United States?

The sixth amendment to the U.S. Constitution ensures the "right of the people to be secure in their persons, houses, papers, and effects," which theoretically means that gays and lesbians are protected by the same legal rights as heterosexuals against crime. Some rights, however, are not afforded to gays and lesbians. Although many states prohibit discrimination on the basis of sexual orientation, that practice is not nationwide. Currently, just 16 states and the District of Columbia have antidiscrimination laws in place. No federal law prohibits discrimination against gays and lesbians in employment and/or housing.

Because the gay rights issue is so controversial, few politicians are willing to speak out on behalf of gays and lesbians. As Larry Kramer, the founder of the advocacy and protest organization AIDS Coalition to Unleash Power (ACT UP), explains: "There is not a candidate or major public figure who would not sell gays down the river. We have seen this time after time, even from supposedly progressive politicians."[4]

Is Homosexuality Genetic?

Gay rights advocates maintain that sexual orientation, like race or gender, is genetic and cannot be changed or "cured." They point to the American

Psychiatric Association's declaration that it is a normal deviation from heterosexuality, which is why the group dropped homosexuality from its list of mental illnesses. Although scientific research has not conclusively proved that sexual orientation is genetic, studies have shown that from a very young age, most children identify with either the same sex or opposite sex in different ways. Whether homosexuality is biological or cultural, or perhaps a combination of both, the issue is of interest to scientists. Many believe that sexual orientation is unlikely to be caused by a single factor, such as a "gay gene," as has been theorized in the past. Rather, homosexuality is likely to be the result of multiple factors, including genetics, relationships with family, childhood experiences, and cultural influence.

> **Currently, just 16 states and the District of Columbia have antidiscrimination laws in place.**

The AIDS Epidemic and Gay Rights

Prior to the 1980s, the deadly disease called acquired immunodeficiency syndrome (AIDS) was virtually unheard of in the United States. The issue first came to light in 1981, when a mysterious, grave illness began afflicting gay men. The disease destroyed their immune systems and resulted in slow, painful death. It was assumed to be some sort of virus but no one knew what it was or what caused it. Health officials concluded that because it almost exclusively struck gay men, it was likely spread through anal intercourse. It was not until 1984, after AIDS had become a public health crisis and thousands of lives were lost, that the cause was announced: the human immunodeficiency virus, or HIV.

The AIDS epidemic was a massive setback for the gay rights movement. After years of steady progress on behalf of the cause, the movement was badly tainted. Some states began to revoke gay rights laws, and a Gallup poll showed that 37 percent of the public had a more negative opinion of gays and lesbians than they had before the extensive publicity about AIDS. The late Jerry Falwell, who founded a group that he called the Moral Majority, was quoted as saying, "AIDS is the wrath of a just God against homosexuals."[5]

Gays and Lesbians in the Military

One of the most contentious issues among gays and lesbians is the U.S. military's policy about gay and lesbian soldiers. In 1981 the U.S. De-

These gay veterans march in Oakland on Veterans Day to protest the military's Don't Ask, Don't Tell policy. In 1993 Congress passed Don't Ask, Don't Tell, which held that even though gays and lesbians were officially not allowed to serve in the armed forces, their service would be tolerated as long as they did not make their sexual orientation known, did not act on it, and did not talk about it while they were in the military.

partment of Defense adopted a ban on gays and lesbians that led to numerous discharges from military service. When Bill Clinton was elected president in 1992, he promised to end discrimination against gays and lesbians in the military. A report released in July 2008 by retired military officers explains: "Clinton framed his position in terms of 'meritocracy,' saying that the nation could not afford to exclude capable citizens from helping their country even if some citizens did not like them."[6] Clinton, however, met with fierce opposition from Congress, military officials, and politicians, so he agreed to study the issue further. In 1993 Congress passed the Don't Ask, Don't Tell policy, which held that even though gays and lesbians were officially not allowed to serve in the armed forces, their service would be tolerated as long as they did not make their sexual orientation known, did not act on it, and did not talk about it while they were in the military. Clinton supported the policy and signed it into law, which infuriated gays and lesbians who believed that they were being unfairly discriminated against. Their anger and frustration over this policy persists today, and gay rights groups say that one of their biggest priorities is to get the policy changed.

> " The AIDS epidemic was a massive setback for the gay rights movement. "

Even some military officials agree that the Don't Ask, Don't Tell policy is antiquated, discriminatory, and inappropriate. That is the perspective of Josh Gibbs, who is a retired captain with the U.S. Marine Corps. In an article entitled "It's Time to Allow Gays to Serve Openly in the Military," Gibbs writes: "Why do we still cling to the as-yet unproven notion that if gay men and women are allowed to serve openly, unit cohesion and morale would suffer? This assertion is an insult to the professionalism of the U.S. military and an affront to our Constitution."[7] Gibbs compares the policy to racial and sexual discrimination:

> There was a time when allowing blacks to serve in the military was considered prejudicial to good order and discipline. That time has passed, and it is hard to imagine our military without their sacrifice and dedication. There was also a time when the idea of women serving the military in any capacity was unthinkable. Today, women are viewed as equals to men in all but the most physically demanding military specialties. Yet we still drag our heels over the matter of sexual orientation.[8]

Gibbs's superiors were not happy with him for writing the article. After nine years in the Marines, he was relieved of duty due to his commanding officer's "loss of confidence" in his ability.

Harassment

Throughout history gays and lesbians have been the target of harassment, anger, and/or violent acts committed by people who had no tolerance for their sexual orientation. Even though progress has been made in gay rights, gays and lesbians still often face harassment. Terrance McGeorge, a black gay man from Pennsylvania, shares his thoughts on this: "Oh my God, I think maybe four or five times a week I'm getting called 'faggot.' I can't go into a store to buy cigarettes without being told I'm a 'faggot' and I'm going to hell. I can't get on a bus without someone getting in my face. Sometimes the discrimination hurts, but I'm unapologetic for who I am. I won't apologize and I won't change for anyone."[9]

In June 2008 a gay police officer from Huntington Beach, California, received a large financial settlement from the city after he filed harassment charges. Adam Bereki, who had been with the police force since 2001, said that he was taunted and harassed by fellow officers. His attorney explains: "They really relentlessly harassed and ridiculed him. They made his life miserable and he couldn't tolerate it anymore."[10] One of his peers reportedly said in front of supervisors that Bereki only handled gay sex crimes and would make a great cross-dresser, as well as alleging that a visit to his doctor was the result of his being infected with HIV. As a result of the lawsuit, Bereki received a $150,000 lump sum settlement from the city and will also receive disability payments of $4,000 per month for the rest of his life.

> Some military officials agree that the Don't Ask, Don't Tell policy is antiquated, discriminatory, and inappropriate.

Should Gays and Lesbians Have the Legal Right to Marry?

On September 21, 1996, Bill Clinton signed into law the Defense of Marriage Act, which explicitly defined marriage as a union between a man

This lesbian couple celebrates California's Supreme Court ruling in May 2008 that allows same-sex couples to marry. California and Massachusetts are the only two states that legally recognize such unions.

and a woman. Although it did not make same-sex marriage illegal, it gave states the right to refuse recognition of it. Gays and lesbians were infuriated. Why, they asked, were they being discriminated against in such a way? Why were they singled out by the government? Advocates of gay rights said then, and maintain today, that gays and lesbians should have the same right to marry as heterosexuals, without government interference.

As of October 2008 only 2 states allowed gays and lesbians to legally marry: Massachusetts (since 2004) and California (since 2008). In every other state homosexual marriage is against the law, although some have domestic partnership legislation in place. The Bush administration has tried to get same-sex marriage banned through a constitutional amendment, but to date that effort has failed.

Should Gays and Lesbians Raise Children?

Many people who oppose same-sex relationships are especially adamant about prohibiting gays and lesbians from becoming parents, either through in vitro fertilization or adoption. The most common argument is that children need both a mother and a father, and it is not good for them to be raised in a nontraditional family. In a December 12, 2006, *Time* magazine article, Focus on the Family's James C. Dobson addressed this issue. He specifically referred to Mary Cheney (daughter of former Vice President Dick Cheney), who is raising her biological son with her lesbian partner Heather Poe. Dobson cited "more than 30 years of social-science evidence" showing that children are much better off when they are raised by a mother and father who are married. "That is not to say Cheney and Poe will not love their child," he wrote. "But love alone is not enough to guarantee healthy growth and development. The two most loving women in the world cannot provide a daddy for a little boy—any more than the two most loving men can be complete role models for a little girl."[11]

A number of people do not share Dobson's perspective. They argue that no studies conclusively prove that children are harmed in any way by being raised by loving, devoted gay and lesbian parents. This is the perspective of Kyle Pruett of Yale University, who was cited in Dobson's article as believing that children of gay or lesbian parents may suffer developmentally. Pruett was furious, and when he was unable to contact Dobson, he taped an interview denouncing him and posted it on YouTube. He explains:

> Look, I said, if you're going to use my research to judge and implicate personal decisions people are making, you are going to hear from me about it because I consider this a destructive use of good science. While fathers make unique contributions to children, never do I say in my book that children of gay parents are at risk. Love binds parents and children together, not gender. There are plenty of boys and girls from these families with masculine and feminine role models who turn out just fine.[12]

What Is the Future of Gay Rights?

Because of the growing strength of gay rights groups, as well as the support of powerful advocacy organizations such as the American Civil Liberties

Union (ACLU), gays and lesbians have made strides in their fight for equal rights. Yet in spite of the progress that has been made over the years, gays and lesbians are still not afforded equal rights with heterosexuals. In all but two states they cannot legally marry, and a few states prohibit same-sex couples from adopting children. Gays and lesbians are not protected on a federal level from discrimination by employers or landlords, nor are they given protection from hate crimes. If they serve in the military, they must keep their sexual orientation secret or face discharge. And even though sodomy laws have been declared unconstitutional, some states still uphold their own laws and make arrests for what they claim to be sodomy violations. For these reasons, gay rights advocates vow to keep working toward the time when they are treated equally and fairly. "Throughout history," writes Gibbs, "America has been at the forefront of the war against intolerance. . . . Why, then, have we not led the charge in this fight? . . . There comes a time when people must stand up in the face of intolerance and push this country forward for the good of future generations. Now is the time to stand. Now is the time to push."[13]

> " In spite of the progress that has been made over the years, gays and lesbians are still not afforded equal rights with heterosexuals. "

Are Gay Rights Protected in the United States?

66 I have a hard time . . . understanding why there's a segment of the population obsessed with preventing homosexuals from enjoying equal treatment here in the land of the free. 99

—D. Allan Kerr, "Prediction: Gay Marriage Will Be Protected Under Constitution."

66 The majority of our legislators have chosen to believe the lie that those who engage in homosexual activity cannot help themselves, and that they are being unjustly and wrongly discriminated against, when in fact, neither is true. 99

—David Crowe, quoted in Bob Unruh, "'Gay'-Rights Bill Lets Court Define Church's 'Purpose.'"

In the United States, discrimination on the basis of race, religion, gender, color, or national origin is prohibited under civil rights laws that were passed during the 1960s. For instance, it is illegal for people to be discriminated against when they are in the workplace, seek employment promotions, vote in elections, attend the theater, visit restaurants, or stay in hotels or motels. They are also protected under civil rights legislation when they attend school, buy a house, or rent an apartment. These laws do not apply to everyone in the United States, however. The only federal law that protects gays and lesbians is Executive Order 13087, which was signed by Bill Clinton in 1998 and prohibits discriminatory practices based on sexual orientation in federal civilian hiring. Unless states have their own civil rights legislation in place, many types of discrimination against gays and lesbians remain legal under federal law.

State and Municipal Laws

As of October 2008 fewer than half of the 50 U.S. states had laws in place to protect gays and lesbians from discrimination. The eastern states with such laws are Connecticut, Maryland, Massachusetts, New Hampshire, New Jersey, New York, Pennsylvania, Rhode Island, and Vermont. The western states are California, Colorado, Iowa, Nevada, Oregon, and Washington, while the remainder include Hawaii, Illinois, Minnesota, and Wisconsin, as well as the District of Columbia.

> " Unless states have their own civil rights legislation in place, many types of discrimination against gays and lesbians remain legal under federal law. "

In Oregon gays and lesbians are protected by the Oregon Equality Act, which was approved by the state senate and signed by the governor in 2007. The law prohibits discrimination in housing, employment, public accommodations, education, and public services statewide; and it passed by a wide margin of votes, 19 to 7. One Oregon legislator who did not vote in favor of the act, and who is adamantly against it, is Senator Gary George of Salem. Almost immediately after the law was passed, George began working to repeal it. He and his supporters, however, were not able to gather enough signatures for it to be put on the November 2007 ballot, and the law took effect on January 1, 2008. In an interview a few months later, George was asked to share his views about the Oregon Equality Act's safeguards against people being fired from jobs because of their sexual orientation. "As an employer, I don't wanna' hear about it," he replied. "This workplace is for work purposes. My advice to the gay community is shut up, just don't talk about it. If you walk around talking about what you do in the bedroom, you should be on the pervert channel."[14]

One area of the country where antidiscrimination laws are virtually nonexistent is the Deep South. In Alabama and Mississippi, for instance, gays and lesbians can legally be fired from their jobs, as well as prevented from eating in a restaurant, staying at a luxury resort, or enrolling in college. The same is true in Arkansas, Florida, Texas, and Louisiana, as well as other southern states. In some cases, though, municipalities have passed their own civil rights laws despite the lack of state legislation. One example is Columbia, the capital of South Carolina, which in 2008 became the first city in the state to enact laws that protect gays and lesbians. Only two other cities in the Deep South, Atlanta and New Orleans, have such civil rights laws in place, although several hundred municipalities throughout the country have passed antidiscrimination laws. One example is Dayton, Ohio, which in November 2007 became the fifteenth city in Ohio to add "sexual orientation" to its list of protected groups.

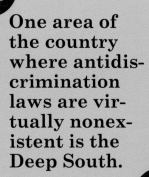

One area of the country where antidiscrimination laws are virtually nonexistent is the Deep South.

Discrimination in School

The First Amendment of the United States Constitution protects people's rights to speak freely, as it states: "Congress shall make no law . . . abridging the freedom of speech, or of the press." But in states that have no antidiscrimination laws in place, even children can be punished for what they say or do. In November 2003 a 7-year-old Louisiana boy named Marcus McLaurin was in line for recess when a classmate asked about his parents. Marcus explained that he had two mothers because his own mother was gay, and when he was asked what that meant, Marcus said "gay is when a girl likes another girl."[15] He was scolded by his teacher, sent to the principal's office, and given a "Student Behavior Contract" to take home for his mother to sign. On the document, his teacher had written why Marcus was being disciplined: "He explained to another child that you are gay (underlined twice), and what gay means."[16] Marcus's mother had previously received a telephone call from the school's assistant principal, who said that her son was in trouble for using such a bad word that it could not be repeated on the phone. But that call, she later said, "was nothing compared to the shock I felt when my little boy came home and told me that his teacher had told him his family is a dirty word."[17] Marcus was also required to attend a one-hour disciplinary "behavior clinic," during which he was made to write repeatedly, "I will never use the word 'gay' in school again."[18]

In April 2007 a gay high school student from Jonesborough, Tennessee, was also the victim of discrimination. Curtis Walsh, who at the time was a senior at David Crockett High School, had helped organize and participate in a silent demonstration to raise awareness about antigay violence. When he arrived at school on April 18, he was immediately called to the principal's office and told that he would be suspended from school for three days for his participation in the event. Walsh, who stated that he had been a frequent target of antigay harassment at his school, explains his frustration over the punishment: "I just wanted to do something positive about the harassment I've had to deal with every day at this school. I'm graduating in a few days, but I want things to be better for future gay students than they were for me. It's pretty ironic that my principal decided to silence me for taking part in a protest in which I was planning to be silent all day."[19]

Military Discrimination

Bill Clinton's executive order of 1998 affords federal employees protection from discrimination despite their sexual orientation, but this only applies to civilian employees, not those in the military. Gays and lesbians are bound to obey the Don't Ask, Don't Tell policy, and if they do not, they are subject to immediate discharge no matter how high they are in rank, how long they have served, or how decorated they are. In November 2004 Air Force major Margaret Witt was stunned to learn that she had been the target of an investigation because of her involvement in a lesbian relationship from 1997 to 2003. In keeping with military policy, Witt had not told anyone of her sexual orientation, nor was she open about it. Over her 19 years of service as an operating room and flight nurse she had

> " In May 2008 the U.S. Court of Appeals ruled that the Air Force needed to show just cause for discharging [Officer Majorie] Witt. "

received numerous commendations, including an Air Force Commendation Medal for saving the life of a Department of Defense worker, and the Air Medal awarded to her by President Bush. But because her lesbianism was discovered, she was discharged. The officer who gave her the news said to go quietly and not tell anyone about it. She was told that she could no longer report for duty, no longer be paid, no longer earn points toward retirement, and that she had been stripped of her promotion to lieutenant colonel. Witt was devastated, and she contacted the American Civil Liberties Union (ACLU), who represented her in a discrimination lawsuit. In May 2008 the U.S. Court of Appeals ruled that the Air Force needed to show just cause for discharging Witt by proving that her behavior had actually harmed morale or jeopardized the military's interest. The court emphasized that "generalized or hypothetical assertions about the impact of gay and lesbian service members would not be sufficient."[20] Witt explains her happiness at hearing the verdict: "I am thrilled by the court's recognition that I can't be discharged without proving that I was harmful to morale. I want to serve my country. I have loved being in the military—my fellow airmen have been my family. I am proud of my career and want to continue doing my job. Wounded people never asked me about my sexual orientation. They were just glad to see me there."[21]

The Hate Crime Controversy

According to the FBI, hate crimes are motivated by biases based on race, religion, sexual orientation, ethnicity/national origin, and disability. In 2006 more than 9,500 people in the United States were victims of hate crimes, of which 1,472 involved sexual orientation. These sorts of crimes are reported and prosecuted just like other criminal activities, but hate crimes often result in more severe punishment because they are a violation of federal hate crime legislation. Yet even though gays and lesbians are often the target of hate crimes, the law does not protect them because its wording contains no reference to sexual orientation. In May 2007 the U.S. House of Representatives voted to change that by passing a bill entitled the Local Law Enforcement Hate Crimes Prevention Act. Six months later the Senate passed a similar bill entitled the Matthew Shepard Local Law Enforcement Hate Crimes Prevention Act of 2007.

The Senate's version of the hate crime legislation was named after the victim of a heinous hate crime that was committed in 1998. On a cold October night a 21-year-old gay college student named Matthew Wayne Shepard was brutally beaten and tortured by 2 men near Laramie, Wyoming. After the beating the attackers tied Shepard to a fence and left him there to die. Eighteen hours passed before an onlooker spotted him hanging on the fence and initially thought the young man was a scarecrow. Shepard was rushed to the hospital where doctors found that the beating had caused severe brain damage. After 5 days of hospitalization, Shepard died. Writer and gay rights activist Andrew Sullivan describes the aftermath of Shepard's attack and death among the gay and lesbian community: "I think a lot of gay people, when they first heard of that horrifying event, felt sort of punched in the stomach. I mean it kind of encapsulated all our fears of being victimized."[22] A year after the attack Shepard's murderers, Aaron McKinney and Russell Henderson, were convicted and sentenced to double life sentences in prison.

> " On a cold October night a 21-year-old gay college student named Matthew Wayne Shepard was brutally beaten and tortured by 2 men near Laramie, Wyoming. "

As tragic as Shepard's death was, it received widespread media publicity and sparked outrage among Americans. This increased awareness put hate crimes in the spotlight and led to a national debate over hate crime legislation. The result was the decision by federal politicians to include sexual orientation along with race, religion, color, and national origin. Yet this is an issue of controversy, as many people disagree that sexual orientation should be included in the law. In fact, some believe that hate crime legislation should not exist at all. Their viewpoint is that laws already exist to protect people against violent crime, and hate crime laws single out specific groups and treat their crimes as more serious than others. Robert Knight, the director of the Culture and Media Institute, explains: "In a media- and dollar-driven situation, your grandmother's mugging will not receive as much attention as the 'hate crime' committed against a homosexual. Both victims deserve the full protection of the law, but the one that snags the headlines will get more of it."[23]

An Ongoing Battle

Gay rights has been an issue of debate for decades. Although it would appear that much progress has been made, gays and lesbians still face discrimination and harassment on a daily basis. Students are taunted by classmates and sometimes suspended from school for speaking openly about homosexuality. Soldiers are discharged by the military because of their sexual orientation, and in most states gays and lesbians can be fired from their jobs or denied housing. Striving to be treated equally and have the same rights as heterosexuals is an ongoing battle for them, yet they believe the effort is well worth it. As *Chicago Free Press* writer Jennifer Vanasco explains: "Liberty means freedom, and we now understand that freedom is the ability to have full political agency, whether you're male or female, black or white, gay or straight. To be an American is to exercise this agency. To be a gay American is to remind others that there is nothing more American than fighting for our fundamental rights."[24]

Primary Source Quotes*

Are Gay Rights Protected in the United States?

66Once again, we are at a place in our society where we are, some are, looking at a small minority of people, gay and lesbian families, and saying you are not deserving as the same as the rest of society.99

—Cheryl Jacques, "Gay Marriage," *Online NewsHour*, PBS, February 13, 2004. www.pbs.org.

Jacques was the first openly gay state senator in Massachusetts history and is the former president of the Human Rights Campaign.

66As a Black woman who happens to be an alumnus of the University of Toledo's Graduate School, an employee and business owner, I take great umbrage at the notion that those choosing the homosexual lifestyle are 'civil rights victims.'99

—Crystal Dixon, "Gay Rights and Wrongs: Another Perspective," *Toledo Free Press*, April 18, 2008. www.toledofreepress.com.

Dixon, formerly associate vice president for human resources at the University of Toledo, was fired after writing this column.

Bracketed quotes indicate conflicting positions.

* Editor's Note: While the definition of a primary source can be narrowly or broadly defined, for the purposes of Compact Research, a primary source consists of: 1) results of original research presented by an organization or researcher; 2) eyewitness accounts of events, personal experience, or work experience; 3) first-person editorials offering pundits' opinions; 4) government officials presenting political plans and/or policies; 5) representatives of organizations presenting testimony or policy.

66 I, for one, will not be excluded from my Catholic faith or church by leadership that is grounded in a selective interpretation of scripture, tradition and theological discourse or that is focused on a preoccupation with condemning the loving human relationships of gay and lesbian children of God. 99

—Brad Huard, "Homosexual Lifestyles," *National Catholic Reporter,* December 28, 2007.

Huard is a gay man from Edina, Minnesota.

66 If you don't believe in Church teaching, move on. There are all sorts of other churches who do not care what you believe and various liberal Protestant churches that now enthusiastically endorse homosexuality. . . . But don't criticize the Catholic Church for being Catholic. 99

—Michael Coren, "Giuliani's Public Hyprocisy," *Catholic Insight,* December 2007.

Coren is an author, broadcaster, and newspaper columnist.

66 The problem with being different is that people don't like it. Gay lyricist Howard Ashman puts it best in a song for his *Beauty and the Beast* score: As peasants head out with pitchforks, they sing, 'We don't like what we don't understand, in fact it scares us.' 99

—Beren deMotier, "Out with My Son," *Curve,* May 2008.

DeMotier is a freelance writer from Portland, Oregon.

❝Homosexuality, delivered to young minds, is by its very nature pornographic. It destroys impressionable minds and confuses their developing sexuality.❞

—Michael Glatze, "How a 'Gay Rights' Leader Became Straight," *WorldNet Daily*, July 3. 2007. www.wnd.com.

Glatze, the former publisher of *Young Gay America* magazine who now renounces homosexuality, believed that he was gay from the time he was 14 years old until he was 30.

❝For many of us, living quietly within the confines of the mothball-infested closet is like being trapped in one of those space-bags of winter clothes; we're deflated with the life sucked out of us, waiting for a better time and hoping for more seasonable weather to open up into freedom.❞

—Kate Lacey, "Coming Out to Your Parents," *Curve*, October 2007.

Lacey is a writer for the lesbian magazine *Curve*.

❝I really believe that the pagans and the abortionists and the feminists and the gays and the lesbians, who are actively trying to make that an alternative lifestyle . . . I point the finger in their face and say, 'You helped this [9/11 terrorist attack] happen.'❞

—Jerry Falwell, quoted in David Molpus, "Televangelist, Christian Leader Jerry Falwell Dies," *All Things Considered*, NPR, May 15, 2007. www.npr.org.

Falwell, who was vehemently against homosexuality, founded an organization he called the Moral Majority in 1979.

66 For now, in the United States, speech against homo-sexuality is not itself being prosecuted as a hate crime because the First Amendment is being used to defeat such measures. 99

—"Punishing People Who Have a Viewpoint," *The New American*, August 6, 2007.

The New American is a conservative biweekly publication that is published by a subsidiary of the John Birch Society.

66 But the thing about staying in the closet is, you're constantly lying—making up excuses for not having a boyfriend, and it sucks. Neither Sarah nor I was out. We lived in a bubble, hiding from the world, ashamed of our relationship. 99

—Deborah Baer, "The Story of My Coming Out," *CosmoGirl,* April 2008.

Baer is an entertainment writer and editor.

66 One of the most transformative social movements over our lifetime has been the battle for gay rights, and the key to its great success has been the grass-roots phe-nomenon of exploding stereotypes by simply saying, 'Yes, I am.' 99

—Anna Quindlen, "The Same People," *Newsweek,* June 9, 2008. www.newsweek.com.

Quindlen is a Pulitzer prize–winning journalist and author who lives in New York City.

66 Conservatives are using Christian rhetoric to justify discrimination against lesbian, gay, bisexual, and transgender (LGBT) people. **99**

—Kittridge Cherry, "Take Back Jesus," *Tikkun*, March/April 2008.

Cherry is a lesbian minister and art historian.

66 I understand why Christians resent being called bigots and haters. I get why they oppose homosexuality. I get it. But please, if there is a war between Christians and homosexuals, it's their war, not ours. **99**

—Jim David, "Antigay and Proud," *Advocate*, January 29, 2008.

David is a comedian and writer who often appears on the television show *Comedy Central*.

Facts and Illustrations

Are Gay Rights Protected in the United States?

- No federal legislation gives gays and lesbians **equal protection** under the law in employment, housing, schooling, or public accommodations.

- In 1981 Wisconsin became the first state to pass a law **prohibiting discrimination** against homosexuals in the workplace, housing, or public accommodations.

- In 1982 a federal judge ruled that the policy of the United States Immigration and Naturalization Service to exclude gays and lesbians from entering the United States was **unconstitutional**.

- According to the **Don't Ask, Don't Tell policy**, gays and lesbians can serve in the military as long as they do not reveal their sexual orientation or engage in homosexual acts.

- **Massachusetts** was the first state to prohibit discrimination against gay and lesbian students in public schools.

- In 2000 the U.S. Supreme Court ruled that the **Boy Scouts of America** could ban gay men from serving as troop leaders.

- Since 2003 **sodomy laws have been unconstitutional** in the United States.

- **Thirty** U.S. states have no antidiscrimination legislation in place.

Sexual-Orientation Antidiscrimination Laws

Under federal law, people in the United States are protected from discrimination based on race, religion, sex, color, or national origin, but not sexual orientation (with the exception of federal civilian employees). This map shows which states have sexual-orientation antidiscrimination laws in place.

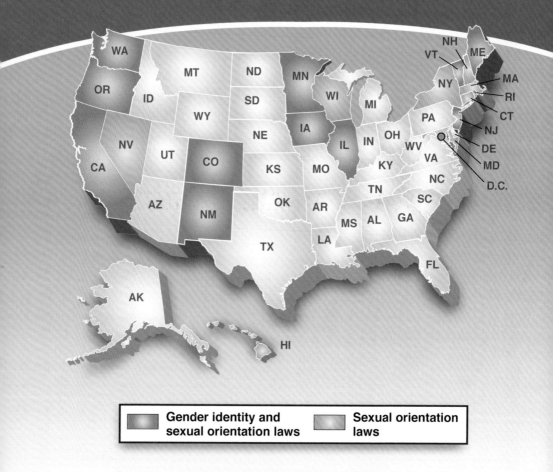

Gender identity and sexual orientation laws

Sexual orientation laws

Source: Human Rights Campaign Foundation, "The State of the Workplace for Gay, Lesbian, Bisexual, and Transgender Americans," 2007. www.hrc.org.

- The first gay rights march on Washington, D.C., was held in October 1979 and drew an estimated **75,000** people.

- **The Briggs Initiative**, which would have barred gays and lesbians from teaching in public schools, was defeated in 1978 and was considered a major victory for the gay rights movement.

- Current **hate crime legislation** does not apply to gays and lesbians.

- The passage of the **Hate Crime Statistics Act in 1989** ensured that hate crimes against gays and lesbians would be tracked by the FBI.

Harassment in Schools

According to a study published in 2008 by the Gay, Lesbian, and Straight Education Network, many young people in the United States are victims of harassment and/or assault while they are at school. This graph shows a breakdown of why these students report being targeted.

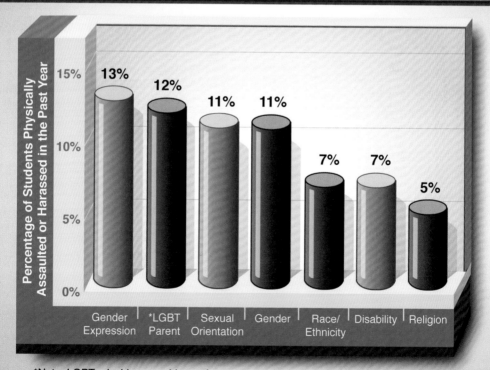

*Note: LGBT = lesbian, gay, bisexual, or transgender.

Source: Gay, Lesbian, and Straight Education Network, "Involved, Invisible, Ignored," 2008. www.glsen.org.

"Don't Ask, Don't Tell" Policy

Prior to 1993 gays and lesbians were banned from serving in any branch of the United States military. Once the Don't Ask, Don't Tell policy went into effect, homosexuals could serve as long as they did not talk about their sexual orientation or act on it. Even with the policy in place, thousands of gay and lesbian military personnel have been discharged since the 1990s, although it has steadily declined in recent years.

Number of gays and lesbians discharged from the military since Don't Ask, Don't Tell took effect

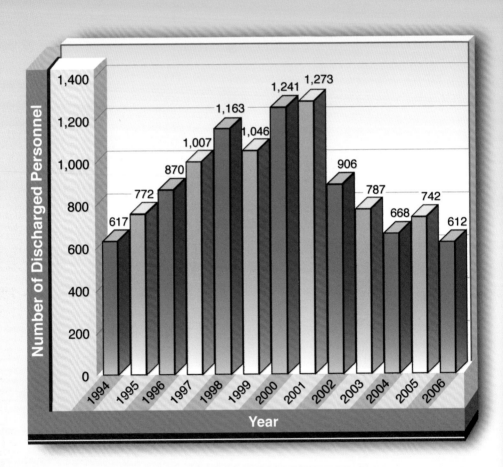

Source: Public Agenda, "Military Discharges," Gay Rights: Fact File, 2007. www.publicagenda.org.

Americans' Views on Gay Rights and Employment

Public opinion about employment discrimination has changed radically over the years. In a May 2008 Gallup poll, 89 percent of respondents said that gays and lesbians should have equal rights in terms of job opportunities, compared to 56 percent in 1977, as these charts show.

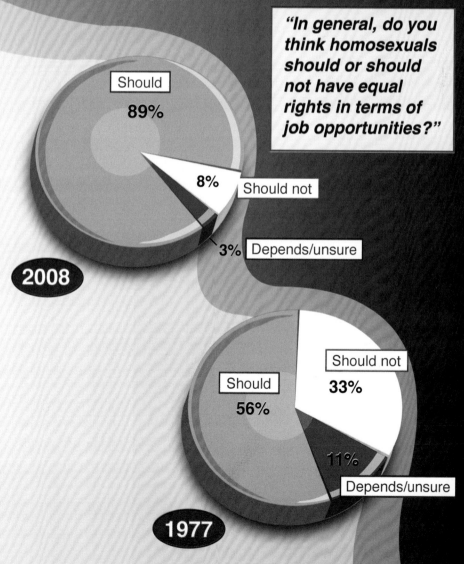

"In general, do you think homosexuals should or should not have equal rights in terms of job opportunities?"

Should
89%

8% Should not

3% Depends/unsure

2008

Should not
33%

Should
56%

11%

Depends/unsure

1977

Source: PollingReport.com, "Law and Civil Rights," Gallup Poll, May 8–11, 2008. www.pollingreport.com.

Should Gays and Lesbians Have the Legal Right to Marry?

66 **The desire on the part of gay couples to be married is not simply about fairness, but about being seen and recognized as people like all others, who share the capacity to love deeply and experience profound intimacy and unquestioned commitment.** 99

—Peter Clothier, "Gay Marriage: Personal Freedoms and Equal Rights."

66 **Homosexuality and homosexual civil marriage would rip the fabric of society in ways that may be difficult, if not impossible, to mend.** 99

—Peter Sprigg, "Homosexuality: The Threat to the Family and the Attack on Marriage."

May 15, 2008, was a day of joy and celebration for gays and lesbians in California. In a four-to-three vote, the state supreme court struck down laws that had limited marriages to unions between a man and a woman—and in doing so, declared that same-sex couples have a constitutional right to marry. The court stated that a person's ability to establish a loving, long-term, committed relationship with someone else was not dependent on sexual orientation, nor was sexual orientation a legitimate basis on which to deny the right of marriage. After the decision was announced in San Francisco, people who had waited for hours rejoiced over the news. Geoff Kors, director of the gay rights advocacy group Equality California, shares his thoughts: "Today will go down as a true turning point. It really is a very powerful message that love trumps hate and hope trumps fear." [25]

A Decades-Long Courtship

Phyllis Lyon and Del Martin met in 1950 in Seattle, when they were both editors for the *Pacific Builder and Engineer* trade magazine. Within a few years they had fallen in love, and in 1953 they moved to San Francisco. They visited lesbian bars on occasion, but they did not do it often because of the known risk of police raids and inevitable arrest. They decided to form their own social club for lesbians, and in 1955, along with 6 other women, Lyon and Martin founded the Daughters of Bilitis. After a year had passed they grew tired of limiting their organization to a secretive social group, and they decided to expand it into more of a political direction that focused on homosexual rights. Daughters of Bilitis sister groups began forming in other cities around the country; by the early 1960s there were more than 200 chapters of the organization. Lyon and Martin became widely known as strong, determined gay rights activists. They helped found an organization for members of the clergy called the Council on Religion and the Homosexual, as well as campaigned for the American Psychiatric Association (APA) to remove homosexuality from its diagnostic manual of mental disorders (*DSM*). They accomplished that goal in 1973 when the APA publicly declared that gays and lesbians were not mentally ill and denounced any discrimination against gays and lesbians.

> **Throughout all the years Lyon and Martin were together, getting married was out of the question because same-sex marriage was against the law.**

Throughout all the years Lyon and Martin were together, getting married was out of the question because same-sex marriage was against the law. That seemed as though it might change in February 2004 when San Francisco mayor Gavin Newsom ordered county officials to issue marriage licenses to same-sex couples. Lyon and Martin were jubilant, and on February 12 they became the first same-sex couple to be married in the city. Their marriage did not last very long, however, and it was not because they split up. A huge political backlash broke out, during which conservative groups railed against same-sex marriages, saying that they were illegal and immoral. Less than 6 months after Lyon and Martin were married, the California Supreme Court ruled that Newsom lacked the authority to issue an order that same-sex people could legally wed. In making that proclamation, the court invalidated not only the marriage of Lyon and Martin but also the marriage of nearly 4,000 other gay and lesbian couples.

The court's decision did not affect Lyon and Martin's long-term relationship. They remained committed to each other and continued to live together. Then in May 2008, when the court ruled that it was illegal for the state to ban same-sex marriage, Lyon and Martin were finally allowed to legally marry. Their ceremony took place on June 16, 2008, at the San Francisco city hall and was officiated by Newsom. Lyon, age 83, and Martin, age 87 and confined to a wheelchair, said their marriage vows once again. Newsom later said that presiding over the ceremony had been a privilege. "I think, today, marriage as an institution has been strengthened. I think, today, marriage has been affirmed."[26]

Did the Court Overstep Its Bounds?

When the California Supreme Court ruled that it was illegal for the state to ban gay marriage, it struck down a piece of legislation known as Proposition 22, which stated that "California law will provide that only a marriage between a man and a woman is valid or recognized in California."[27] The law had been passed by voters on March 7, 2000, with 61.2 percent voting in favor of it and 38.8 percent voting against it. By ruling as it did the court bypassed the majority of the people's wishes—and this sparked enormous controversy as well as outrage. Tony Perkins, president of the Family Research Center in Washington, was one who denounced the verdict, saying that it represented a total disregard for what more than 4 million voters had decided eight years before.

After the court's ruling was made public, J. Matt Barber, cultural issues policy director for the Concerned Women for America (CWA), was infuriated and also denounced the decision. Barber referred to same-sex marriage as "counterfeit" marriage, and wrote in a July 3, 2008, article:

> With its recent 4-3 opinion—which arrogantly presumed to redefine the millennia-old definition of legitimate marriage—the California Supreme Court daftly divined that the

framers of the California Constitution intended—all along, I guess—that Patrick Henry really had a constitutional right to "marry" Henry Patrick. In so doing, four black-robed Dr. Frankensteins have loosed that paradoxical abomination tagged same-sex "marriage" on the countryside.[28]

Carol A. Corrigan was one of the justices who did not vote in favor of the ruling. In her dissenting opinion she stated that although she personally supported gays and lesbians being able to call their unions marriage, the voters did not share her views, and their opinion should prevail. "I, and this court, must acknowledge that a majority of Californians hold a different view, and have explicitly said so by their vote. This court can overrule a vote of the people only if the Constitution compels us to do so. Here, the Constitution does not." Corrigan added that the voters who had passed Proposition 22 had clearly shown that they wanted to "keep the meaning of marriage as it has always been understood in California." She stated that the justices who overturned the legislation acted improperly by overriding the voters' wishes. "The majority . . . does that which it acknowledges it should not do: it redefines marriage because it believes marriage should be redefined. It justifies its decision by finding a constitutional infirmity where none exists. . . . Four votes on this court should not disturb the balance reached by the democratic process, a balance that is still being tested in the political arena."[29]

> " By ruling as it did the court bypassed the majority of the people's wishes—and this sparked enormous controversy as well as outrage. "

The Religious Perspective

Many people who are against same-sex marriage believe the way they do because of their religious faith. They reference holy books such as the Bible, saying that marriage can only be between a man and a woman, and anything other than that is a sin. That is the perspective of prominent religious leaders, as well as a number of conservative organizations and legislators. One who shares that opinion is Kevin McCullough, a

Christian writer and broadcaster from New York City. He maintains that gays and lesbians reject traditional marriage because they are enemies of God, and he shares his theory about why they want to engage in same-sex marriages: "No longer satisfied with practicing the unspeakable perverse sexual pleasures that their hearts seek in private bedrooms, they wish to be able to do so in public." McCullough adds that gays and lesbians are against biblical marriage because in order to achieve it for themselves, they would have to "conform to God's plan for sexuality, and the sinful nature in man is not willing to make such submission and conformity happen.... Radical homosexual activists hate marriage because fundamentally they hate God, and the guilt of both drives them to extremes."[30] McCullough also points out that by pursuing same-sex marriage, gays and lesbians seek to destroy the traditional institution of marriage.

> **Many people who are against same-sex marriage believe the way they do because of their religious faith.**

Should the Government Regulate Same-Sex Marriage?

Surveys have consistently shown that most Americans believe gays and lesbians should be treated fairly and equally. In a May 2008 Gallup poll, 89 percent of respondents said that gays and lesbians should have equal rights in terms of job opportunities, and 57 percent said that they considered homosexuality to be an acceptable alternative lifestyle. In terms of same-sex marriage, Americans' views are slightly different. In a June 2008 poll conducted by *Time* magazine, 42 percent said that gay and lesbian couples should be allowed to legally marry, while 51 percent said they should not, and 7 percent were uncertain. Yet it was clear from their responses that the majority do not want the federal government to regulate gay marriage. When asked if they favored or opposed an amendment to the U.S. Constitution that would ban same-sex couples from marrying, 58 percent opposed such a ban, 36 percent favored it, and 6 percent were not sure.

On February 24, 2004, President George W. Bush gave a speech in which he stressed the importance of the Defense of Marriage Act, which was signed into law by former president Bill Clinton in 1996 and defines marriage as being between one man and one woman. Bush added that "some activist judges and local officials have made an aggressive attempt to redefine marriage," and stated that the only way to "prevent the meaning of marriage from being changed forever" was to enact a constitutional amendment that would ban same-sex marriage. He explained:

> An amendment to the Constitution is never to be undertaken lightly. The amendment process has addressed many serious matters of national concern. And the preservation of marriage rises to this level of national importance. The union of a man and woman is the most enduring human institution, honoring—honored and encouraged in all cultures and by every religious faith. Ages of experience have taught humanity that the commitment of a husband and wife to love and to serve one another promotes the welfare of children and the stability of society.[31]

Despite strong support by Bush, other conservative legislators, and religious organizations, the bill failed because it did not win enough congressional votes. In June 2006 the proposal was again in front of Congress, and once again it failed.

If the amendment's supporters had succeeded in getting it passed, federal law would trump state law, and states would no longer be allowed to implement their own same-sex marriage legislation. Because it failed, though, states remain free to put their own laws in place. As of October 2008 gays and lesbians may legally marry only in California and Massachusetts. Hawaii, Maine, New Hampshire, Connecticut, New Jersey, Oregon, Vermont, and Washington have civil union or domestic partnership laws in

> " When asked if they favored or opposed an amendment to the U.S. Constitution that would ban same-sex couples from marrying, 58 percent opposed such a ban, 36 percent favored it, and 6 percent were not sure. "

place, which afford gay and lesbian couples many or all of the same legal rights of marriage with the exception of the title.

What Is the Fate of Same-Sex Marriage?

Marriage among gays and lesbians is one of the most contentious issues of the gay rights movement. Those who support it say that homosexual couples fall in love and become just as committed to each other as heterosexuals. The opposition's viewpoint is that marriage is sacred and should be restricted to the union of a man and a woman. Religious and other conservative organizations constantly lobby on behalf of a constitutional amendment that would ban same-sex marriage, while gay and lesbian advocacy groups lobby against it. Without such a federal law in place, states may pass their own marriage legislation, and currently same-sex marriage is only legal in two states. Will more states allow it in the future? Will a constitutional ban eventually be passed? No one knows the answers to those questions. What is known is that the supporters, and the opponents, vow that they will not stop fighting until their battle has been won.

Primary Source Quotes*

Should Gays and Lesbians Have the Legal Right to Marry?

Every right, protection, and obligation of marriage should be open to same-sex couples.

—Joe Solmonese, "Same-Sex Marriage Deserves Federal Legalization," *BusinessWeek Debate Room,* April 14, 2008. www.businessweek.com.

Solmonese is president of the Human Rights Campaign, America's largest gay, lesbian, bisexual, and transgender civil rights organization.

The beautiful and special institution of marriage is only for a man and a woman. It's self-evident, natural, and sexually and reproductively true.

—Randy Thomasson, "Preserve Marriage Rights for a Man and Woman," *BusinessWeek Debate Room,* April 14, 2008. www.businessweek.com.

Thomasson is founder and president of Campaign for Children and Families, an organization whose mission is to promote family values and basic moral standards.

Bracketed quotes indicate conflicting positions.

* Editor's Note: While the definition of a primary source can be narrowly or broadly defined, for the purposes of Compact Research, a primary source consists of: 1) results of original research presented by an organization or researcher; 2) eyewitness accounts of events, personal experience, or work experience; 3) first-person editorials offering pundits' opinions; 4) government officials presenting political plans and/or policies; 5) representatives of organizations presenting testimony or policy.

66 Opportunity. Respect. They underlie our whole Western community and self-image. Gay people should be able to marry like anybody else. 99

—Ned Farquhar, "Many Folks Out West Find Gay Marriage Acceptable,"
Albuquerque Journal, June 26, 2008. www.abqjournal.com.

Farquhar is a former senior policy adviser to the governor of New Mexico.

66 We are going against nature and what we all know is true if we accept gay marriage. Two people of the same sex cannot make a marriage. They cannot and never will make a marriage. 99

—Dan Nelson, "Vote Against Gay Marriage," *Ventura County Star,* June 22, 2008. www.venturacountystar.com.

Nelson is a Baptist minister from Camarillo, California.

66 The majority of those who are against same-sex marriage are right-wing religious fundamentalists who abhor same-sex marriage because they see marriage as a religious institution with no flexibility. In doing so, they not only show the contempt held for their fellow human beings, but also show the refusal to follow the greatest commandment—loving one another. 99

—Becky Murtha, "Gay Marriage Phobia Leads Only to the Dark Side,"
Western Herald, September 4, 2007. www.westernherald.com.

Murtha is a student at Western Michigan University who writes for the school newspaper.

"If people who engage in homosexual behavior want to dress up and play house, that's their prerogative, but we shouldn't destroy the institutions of legitimate marriage and family in order to help facilitate a counterfeit."

—Matt Barber, "California Supreme Court Betrays 'We the People' on Marriage," news release, Concerned Women for America (CWA), May 15, 2008. www.cwfa.org.

Barber is CWA's policy director for policy issues.

"As a conservative, I believe the state should stay out of the business of judging which unrelated adults may and may not make a marriage commitment to each other, that when a same-sex couple chooses to marry, we conservatives should value their liberty far more than any personal or religious disagreement with homosexuality."

—Terry L. Garlock, "Conservatives Wrong to Fight Gay Marriage," *Atlanta Journal-Constitution*, June 20, 2008. www.ajc.com.

Garlock is a financial planner from Peachtree City, Georgia, who writes a column for the *Atlanta Journal-Constitution*.

"So-called 'conservative' advocates of same-sex civil marriage are optimistic that legal unions would change homosexuals for the better; it seems far more probable that homosexuals would change marriage for the worst."

—Peter Sprigg, "Homosexuality: The Threat to the Family and the Attack on Marriage," *At the Podium*, Family Research Council, March 29, 2004. www.frc.org.

Sprigg is the Family Research Council's vice president for policy.

66 Gays who seek to marry want the same thing. They're not looking for the right to sleep around. They already have that. It's called dating. 99

—William Saletan, "Don't Do unto Others," *Slate*, March 23, 2006. www.slate.com.

Saletan is a national correspondent for *Slate* and the author of *Bearing Right: How Conservatives Won the Abortion War.*

66 Christians feed the poor for the same reason they reject sex outside heterosexual marriage. Following biblical teachings, we love our neighbors and don't want to see them enslaved to poverty or broken sexuality. 99

—*Christianity Today*, "The Gay Shibboleth," August 2007.

Christianity Today is a conservative Christian publication.

66 Marriage is about children, say some: to which the answer is . . . not always, and permitting gay marriage would not alter that. 99

—*Economist* (U.S.), "The Case for Gay Marriage," February 28, 2004.

The *Economist* is a weekly newspaper that focuses on international politics and business news and opinion.

66*Of course* men who love men and women who love women should be entitled to all the advantages of marriage, legal and financial and ineffable, including the secret handshakes and special discounts on Juicy Juice and minivans.99

—Kurt Andersen, "The Gay-Wedding Present," *New York Magazine,* July 17, 2006. http://nymag.com.

Andersen is an author and a columnist for *New York Magazine.*

Should Gays and Lesbians Have the Legal Right to Marry?

- In a May 2008 Gallup poll, **49 percent** of respondents opposed legal marriage between gays and lesbians, **38 percent** were in favor of it, and **12 percent** were unsure.

- The **Defense of Marriage Act**, which was signed into law by Bill Clinton in 1996, defined marriage as being between one man and one woman and gave states the right to set their own policies.

- As of October 2008 only two states allowed gays and lesbians to **legally marry**.

- **Massachusetts** was the first state to legalize same-sex marriage in 2003; **California** followed in 2008 when the state supreme court ruled that banning same-sex marriage was unconstitutional.

- According to a June 2008 report by the Williams Institute, more than **51,000** same-sex couples in California will marry in the next three years.

- An estimated **67,500** gay and lesbian couples are expected to travel to California from other states so they can be married.

- The spending of resident and out-of-state couples on wedding and travel expenses is expected to generate more than **$683 million** for California's economy.

Should Gays and Lesbians Have the Legal Right to Marry?

- A proposed constitutional amendment that would ban same-sex marriage has been **defeated by Congress** on two different occasions.

- As of 2005, **41 states** had laws in place that banned same-sex marriage.

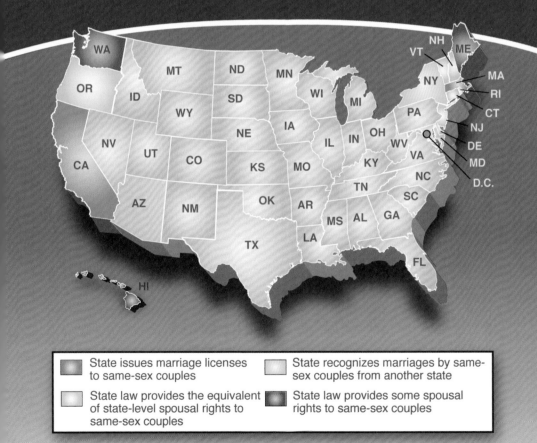

Same-Sex Relationship Recognition

As of October 2008 gays and lesbians could legally marry in only Massachusetts and California. Eight states and the District of Columbia allowed other types of partnerships and rights, but not marriage.

State issues marriage licenses to same-sex couples

State recognizes marriages by same-sex couples from another state

State law provides the equivalent of state-level spousal rights to same-sex couples

State law provides some spousal rights to same-sex couples

Source: Human Rights Campaign Foundation, "The State of the Workplace for Gay, Lesbian, Bisexual, and Transgender Americans," 2007. www.hrc.org.

Economic Impact of Legalizing Same-Sex Marriage in California

In a June 2008 study published by the University of California, Los Angeles Williams Institute, researchers analyzed the impact of increased tourism and wedding-related expenditures on the California economy. These expenditures are expected to result in an enormous increase in state revenues, as this table shows.

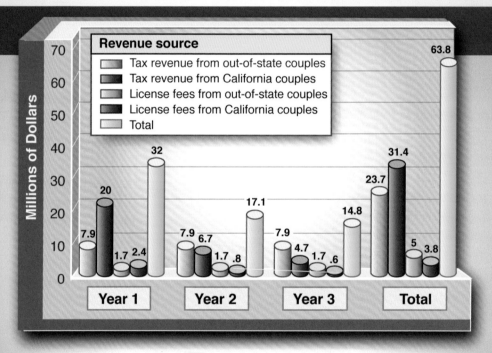

Source: The Williams Institute, "The Impact of Extending Marriage to Same-Sex Couples on the California Budget," June 2008. www.law.ucla.edu.

- An estimated **20 percent** of America's population lives in the seven states that offer same-sex couples broad rights under the law.

- In a July 2008 nationwide survey by Quinnipiac University, the majority of respondents said they **oppose same-sex marriage** but they **do not support a constitutional amendment that would ban it.**

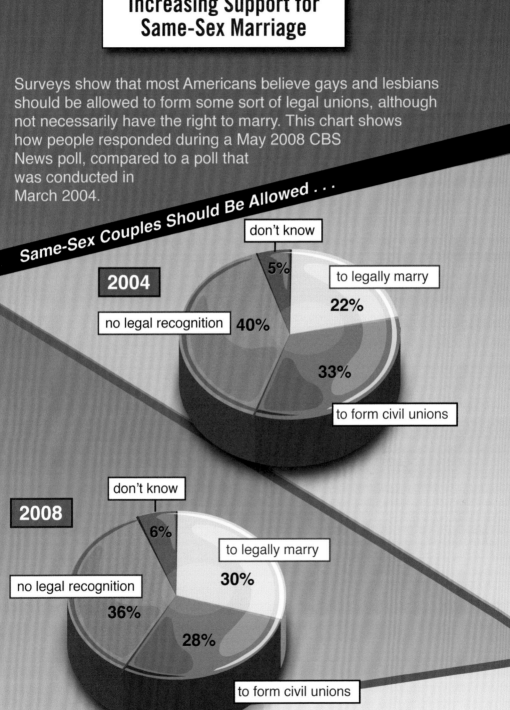

Increasing Support for Same-Sex Marriage

Surveys show that most Americans believe gays and lesbians should be allowed to form some sort of legal unions, although not necessarily have the right to marry. This chart shows how people responded during a May 2008 CBS News poll, compared to a poll that was conducted in March 2004.

Same-Sex Couples Should Be Allowed . . .

2004

don't know
5%

to legally marry
22%

no legal recognition 40%

33%

to form civil unions

2008

don't know
6%

to legally marry
30%

no legal recognition
36%

28%

to form civil unions

Same-Sex Employment Benefits

In 1990 it was virtually unheard of for large companies to provide benefits such as health insurance to domestic partners, but that has begun to change. As of April 2007 nearly 270 Fortune 500 companies offer their employees same-sex domestic partner health benefits.

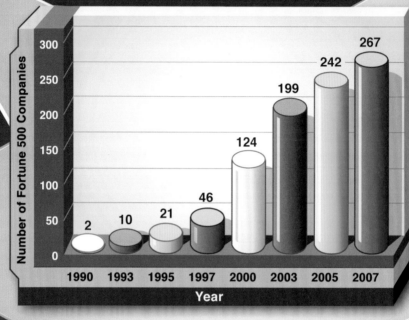

This chart shows which of the Fortune 10 companies provide same-sex domestic health benefits.

Company Name	2006 Fortune Rank
General Motors Corp. (Detroit, MI)	3
Chevron Corp. (San Ramon, CA)	4
Ford Motor Co. (Dearborn, MI)	5
ConocoPhillips (Houston, TX)	6
General Electric Co. (Fairfield, CT)	7
Citigroup Inc. (New York, NY)	8
American International Group Inc. (New York, NY)	9
International Business Machines Corp. (Armonk, NY)	10

Source: Human Rights Campaign Foundation, "The State of the Workplace for Gay, Lesbian, Bisexual, and Transgender Americans," 2007. www.hrc.org.

Should Gays and Lesbians Raise Children?

> 66 Research comparing children raised by homosexual parents to children raised by heterosexual parents has found no developmental differences in intelligence, psychological adjustment, social adjustment, or peer popularity between them. 99

—American Academy of Pediatrics (AAP), "Gay and Lesbian Parents."

> 66 The environment in which children are reared is absolutely critical to their development . . . the American College of Pediatricians believes it is inappropriate, potentially hazardous to children, and dangerously irresponsible to change the age-old prohibition on homosexual parenting, whether by adoption, foster care, or by reproductive manipulation. 99

—American College of Pediatricians (ACP), "Homosexual Parenting: Is It Time for a Change?"

In 2000 Scott Sherman adopted a little boy from an orphanage in Eastern Europe. At the age of 17 months the child, whose name was Sasha, was about the size of a 5-month-old baby. He was sickly, unable to walk, and could barely crawl across the floor. The look in his eyes seemed haunted, and he was withdrawn with no interest in people, toys, or what was going on around him. He did not smile or laugh, nor did he babble or coo, and he did not want to cuddle or for anyone to hold him. Sherman and his partner, Marty Rouse, did not know if they would be able to help their son, but they vowed to try—

and by the time Sasha was 2 years old, the changes in him were nothing short of miraculous. Sherman explains: "By his 2nd birthday, he was grinning and laughing all the time. He went from being severely underweight to downright chubby. He's engaged and affectionate, and every day he wakes up happy. A speech therapist told us that, given Sasha's background, we shouldn't expect any words until 2. But when that birthday arrived, Sasha already had 60 words and phrases. He even says 'please!'"[32]

Everything about their little family seemed perfect until an anonymous person reported Sherman and Rouse for alleged child abuse, and they were investigated by authorities. They later learned the real reason for the report: The woman who made the complaint expressed "how terrible she thought it was that Sasha had two daddies."[33] Despite how much the child had thrived since he was taken out of the orphanage, she was convinced that adoption by a homosexual couple was wrong and should not have been allowed.

Traditional Versus Nontraditional Families

The *American Heritage Dictionary* defines the word *family* as "a fundamental social group in society typically consisting of one or two parents and their children," and "two or more people who share goals and values, have long-term commitments to one another, and reside usually in the same dwelling place."[34] Other dictionaries define it in similar ways. But to those whose personal and/or religious beliefs hold that homosexuality is wrong, the only acceptable family is a traditional one, with both a mother and a father. They are convinced that gays and lesbians are not fit to be parents and should not raise children. This perspective is shared by conservative groups such as Focus on the Family, the Moral Majority, Concerned Women for America, and the Traditional Values Coalition, among others. Their contention is that children raised by same-sex parents do not thrive in the same way as children in traditional families and can be harmed in the process. Bill O'Reilly, the host of the Fox News program *The O'Reilly Factor*, has vehemently denounced gay and lesbian parenting on his show. Some who are opposed to gays and lesbians adopting children, including syndicated radio host Michael Savage, even go so far as to say that it is a form of child abuse for same-sex parents to raise children.

Opponents of gays and lesbians becoming parents often cite research that supports their views, as Focus on the Family's Glenn T. Stanton explains:

> A child needs a loving mother and father. A wealth of research over the past 30 years has shown us this. . . . The most loving mother in the world cannot teach a little boy how to be a man. Likewise, the most loving man cannot teach a little girl how to be a woman. A gay man cannot teach his son how to love and care for a woman. A lesbian cannot teach her daughter how to love a man or know what to look for in a good husband. Is love enough to help two gay dads guide their daughter through her first menstrual cycle? Like a mom, they cannot comfort her by sharing their first experience. Little boys and girls need the loving daily influence of both male and female parents to become who they are meant to be.[35]

Yet according to professional organizations such as the American Academy of Pediatrics, National Association of Social Workers, Child Welfare League of America, American Medical Association, and American Psychiatric Association (APA), the research to which Stanton refers does not exist. They insist that children raised by same-sex parents do just as well, if not better, than children with heterosexual parents. In its 2005 publication *Lesbian & Gay Parenting*, the APA cites numerous studies that have been done throughout the years, all of which refute the idea of gays and lesbians being unfit parents. In its conclusion, the APA writes:

> **Bill O'Reilly, the host of the Fox News program *The O'Reilly Factor*, has vehemently denounced gay and lesbian parenting on his show.**

> There is no evidence to suggest that lesbian women or gay men are unfit to be parents or that psychosocial development among children of lesbian women or gay men is

compromised relative to that among offspring of hetero-sexual parents. Not a single study has found children of lesbian or gay parents to be disadvantaged in any significant respect relative to children of heterosexual parents. Indeed, the evidence to date suggests that home environments provided by lesbian and gay parents are as likely as those provided by heterosexual parents to support and enable children's psychosocial growth.[36]

> " The APA cites numerous studies that have been done throughout the years, all of which refute the idea of gays and lesbians being unfit parents. "

What the Kids Say

In a February 2, 2007, letter to the editor of the *National Catholic Reporter*, a 13-year-old girl named Moriah Ford-Gowan wrote about her family. She had been adopted at the age of 7 by a lesbian couple, and in the years before that she had lived in 7 different foster homes. "If it were not for my moms," she said, "I would probably still be in foster care or, even worse, in a group home."[37] Moriah stated that after the women adopted her they had raised her Catholic, taking her to church, getting her baptized, and arranging for her first communion and confirmation. She decided to write the letter after becoming aware that gays and lesbians were only able to participate in Catholic mass if they kept their sexual orientation secret from other church members, and that it was a sin for them to take holy communion. "I don't see any of this in the Bible or in the teaching of Jesus," she wrote. "Do you?" She went on to say that if everyone was equal in the eyes of God, then everyone should be treated equally, including being able to participate in worship services. "People are people," she wrote. "We are the same: black or white, gay or straight. God created every one of us and we are who we are."[38]

Rebecca Meiksin, a young woman from Ohio, was raised by her biological mother, who was a lesbian, and her mother's partner. Meiksin is very comfortable talking about her nontraditional family and says that she felt perfectly normal when she was growing up. She also challenges anyone who would say that her upbringing was harmful in any way, because she enjoyed her childhood. "A lot of my mom's friends are gay," she says, "and she's really politically active. She took me to gay pride marches and whatnot. I remember sitting out on the deck at New York New York [a pub] eating french fries while she was at meetings."[39] Meiksin adds that the most important thing for any child who is raised by gay or lesbian parents is that the child is loved by his or her family, as she always knew that she was.

Terrance McGeorge, who is now 21, found out when he was 6 years old that his father was gay. For most of his childhood, McGeorge lived with his heterosexual mother, but he says that his father was always his best friend. He explains: "He always encouraged me and was there for me, for whatever it was, graduations, performances, he was there, immediately."[40] He adds that even though he knew his mother loved him and provided him with everything he needed, she struggled with depression, and he now believes that he would have had a more stable childhood if he had lived with his father. He also wonders if he might be a happier, less conflicted person today if his dad had raised him rather than his mother.

According to Robin Sclafani, a young woman whose mother is a lesbian, one of the most difficult aspects of growing up in a same-sex family is not the parents' sexual orientation but the negative reactions of people who do not approve of it. In order to avoid being ostracized, she did not reveal her mother's sexual orientation to anyone until she was a 20-year-old college student. As a child, even her best friends did not know that her mother was a lesbian, and she carried the secret until she could not stand living a lie any longer. She explains:

> The most common opinion I have heard about homosexuality over the years is, "I don't care what they do behind closed doors, as long as they keep it to themselves and . . . don't have children." So does that mean I am a mistake? That my mother is a bad mother? These were just two of the messages I received growing up. . . . My child mind and heart struggled silently against them, knowing deep inside that my mother loved me, as did her female partner.[41]

State Same-Sex Adoption Laws

Whether gays and lesbians can legally adopt children varies widely from state to state. Most states allow single parents, regardless of their sexual orientation, to adopt children. The only state that prohibits all unmarried couples from adopting is Utah, although gays and lesbians who are single may adopt. In Florida, state law has prohibited gays and lesbians from adopting since 1977, but they are allowed to be foster parents. Gay and lesbian singles in Mississippi are permitted to adopt children, but same-sex couples may not. As of July 2008 a group in Arkansas known as the Family Council Action Committee was working to get legislation passed that would ban gays and lesbians from either adopting children or serving as foster parents, even though the state supreme court has struck down such laws in the past. According to Dahlia Lithwick, a journalist who covers legal affairs for the online magazine *Slate*, Alabama, Georgia, Kentucky, Tennessee, Ohio, and Missouri are all in the process of considering constitutional amendments or laws that would ban adoption by gays or lesbians. She denounces such measures because they ignore children who could potentially benefit from living with loving same-sex families. "These legislative bans fly in the face of both necessity and truth," she writes.

> **Most states allow single parents, regardless of their sexual orientation, to adopt children.**

There are 119,000 children waiting to be adopted in this country, about half of them racial and ethnic minorities. There are about 588,000 children in foster care. Legislators—like a clutch of Ohio Republicans—pushing bans on gay adoption and fostering must argue that it's better for these children to languish in state custody, or bounce from foster home to foster home, than be raised by gay parents. Just as there is no data to support the claim that children raised by married gay parents fare worse than those raised by heterosexual ones, there is no data to suggest that foster care is preferable to gay parenting.[42]

An Unresolved Issue

The question of whether gays and lesbians should become parents has no simple answer because it is such a contentious issue with strong opinions on both sides. People who are opposed to it insist that it is not good for a child to be raised by gays and lesbians, and they contend that research supports their viewpoint. Those with the opposite perspective say that no such research exists and that children who live with loving gay or lesbian parents are just as happy and well adjusted as children raised by heterosexual couples. Family Pride's executive director, Jennifer Chrisler, shares her thoughts:

> " The question of whether gays and lesbians should become parents has no simple answer because it is such a contentious issue with strong opinions on both sides. "

> The fundamental reality is that all parents, regardless of gender or sexual orientation, are linked in a very real way. We want our children to be safe, healthy and happy. . . . If their paramount focus is truly the health and well-being of children, then we invite [people opposed to gay and lesbian adoption] to join our fight to ensure that all loving families are recognized, respected, protected and celebrated.[43]

Primary Source Quotes*

Should Gays and Lesbians Raise Children?

66 Anti-gay prejudice hurts many children. Hundreds of thousands of them need homes. Yet some people would prefer that children be stuck in foster care or institutions rather than live with two loving parents of the same sex. I can't decide if that's more crazy or cruel. 99

—Scott Sherman, "If Our Son Is Happy, What Else Matters?" *Newsweek,* September 16, 2002. www.newsweek.com.

Sherman and his partner, who live in Washington, D.C., adopted a little boy from an orphanage in Eastern Europe.

66 We know that it's in the best interest of children to be raised with a mother and a father. To use children as guinea pigs in radical San Francisco–style social experimentation is deplorable. 99

—J. Matt Barber, "California Supreme Court Betrays 'We the People' on Marriage," news release, Concerned Women for America (CWA), May 15, 2008. www.cwfa.org.

Barber is CWA's policy director for cultural issues.

Bracketed quotes indicate conflicting positions.

* Editor's Note: While the definition of a primary source can be narrowly or broadly defined, for the purposes of Compact Research, a primary source consists of: 1) results of original research presented by an organization or researcher; 2) eyewitness accounts of events, personal experience, or work experience; 3) first-person editorials offering pundits' opinions; 4) government officials presenting political plans and/or policies; 5) representatives of organizations presenting testimony or policy.

Primary Source Quotes

66 **The results of some studies suggest that lesbian mothers' and gay fathers' parenting skills may be superior to those of matched heterosexual couples.** 99

—American Psychological Association (APA), "Gay Parenting," 2005. www.apa.org.

The APA, specifically its Lesbian, Gay, and Bisexual Concerns Office, seeks to reduce prejudice, discrimination, and violence against gay, lesbian, and bisexual people.

66 **The majority of Americans . . . know what marriage is: It's the union of a man and woman. They believe children do best when they have mothers and fathers, male and female role models. There is an ocean of empirical data which supports that proposition.** 99

—Matt Daniels, "Gay Marriage," *Online NewsHour,* PBS, February 13, 2004. www.pbs.org.

Daniels is the founder of Alliance for Marriage.

66 **Branding lesbians and gay men as unfit parents has been one of their most vicious tactics since the dawn of the gay rights movement.** 99

—Paul Cates, "Reporting the Truth About the Science on LGBT Parenting," American Civil Liberties Union (ACLU) LGBT & AIDS Annual Update, 2007. www.aclu.org.

Cates is the ACLU's public education director.

66 In the case of marriage, folks who aren't impressed with a child's need to have both a male and a female parent aren't likely to be swayed by . . . studies that imply what common sense would suggest, that the sexual activity of parents affects their children. **99**

—Richard Kirk, "The Gay Marriage Revolution," *North County Times,* November 8, 2007. www.nctimes.com.

Kirk is a freelance columnist for the *North County Times.*

66 At school, I held my head high, but to be honest, middle school was pretty painful. Kids used the word *gay* to describe anything negative, and their teasing stung. . . . I didn't get why people thought something was wrong with my family. I just wished they could see the truth. **99**

—Marina Gatto, "Coming Out (When Your Parents Are Gay)," *CosmoGirl,* April 2007.

Gatto, the straight daughter of lesbian parents, is a gay rights activist.

66 The problem in our schools is not 'homophobia' but homophilia, the bland, unthinking acceptance of all the nonsense implied or propagated about the homosexual lifestyle. **99**

—Alphonse de Valk, "Media Do Not Want the Truth," *Catholic Insight,* January 2004.

De Valk is the editor of *Catholic Insight* magazine.

"States that don't allow adoption by gays? Violence. Parents who disown their children for being gay or acting too butch for a girl, too fern for a boy? Violence. . . . Lesbian- and gay-headed families who love their children unconditionally? That's love."

—Laura J. Weinstock, "Love Is Not Violence," *Advocate*, July 19, 2005.

Weinstock is the lesbian mother of an adopted daughter from China.

....

"I grew up the child of a mixed-gender marriage that lasted until death parted them, and I could tell you about how good that is for children, and you could pay me whatever you think it's worth."

—Garrison Keillor, "Stating the Obvious," *Salon,* March 14, 2007. www.salon.com.

Keillor is an author and the host of the Minnesota Public Radio show, *A Prairie Home Companion.*

....

"What same-sex marriage advocates have tried to present as a civil rights issue is really a bid for special preferences of the type our society gives to married couples for the very good reason that most of them are raising or have raised children."

—Mary Ann Glendon, "For Better or for Worse?" *Wall Street Journal,* February 25, 2004. www.opinionjournal.com.

Glendon is a law professor at Harvard University.

....

❝If children need protection, it's from the prejudices and lies of many of their parents. Unless they're carefully taught to be bigots, children couldn't care less who's gay and who's not, who has two daddies or none at all.❞

—Bruce C. Steele, "A Tale of Two Zachs," *Advocate,* July 19, 2005.

Steele is the former editor in chief of the *Advocate,* a national gay and lesbian newsmagazine.

Facts and Illustrations

Should Gays and Lesbians Raise Children?

- Most U.S. states allow gays and lesbians to **adopt children**.

- The only state where homosexual adoptions are banned is **Florida**.

- According to a report by the Urban Institute, more than **one in three** lesbians have given birth, and **one in six** gay men have either fathered or adopted a child.

- The Urban Institute says that approximately **65,500** adopted children are living with a gay or lesbian parent.

- The most adopted children living with gay or lesbian parents reside in **California**.

- The Urban Institute says that same-sex couples raising children tend to be **older**, more **educated**, and have **more economic resources** than other adoptive parents.

- An estimated **14,000** foster children are living with gay or lesbian parents.

- **No studies** have ever conclusively proven that children are harmed when they are raised by gay or lesbian parents.

- Professional organizations such as the American Academy of Pediatrics, American Psychiatric Association, and the National Welfare League of America say that **children do just as well** when raised by homosexual parents as those who are raised by heterosexual parents.

State Parenting Laws

Most U.S. states allow gays and lesbians to adopt children, but their laws vary widely. This map shows how the various states legislate adoption by homosexual singles and couples.

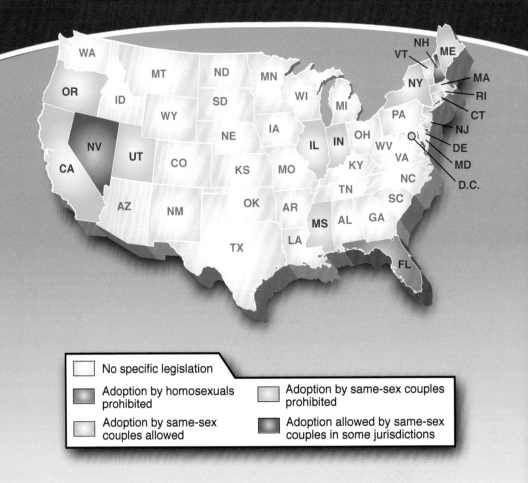

No specific legislation

Adoption by homosexuals prohibited

Adoption by same-sex couples allowed

Adoption by same-sex couples prohibited

Adoption allowed by same-sex couples in some jurisdictions

Source: Human Rights Campaign Foundation, "Parenting Laws in the U.S.," January 9, 2008. www.hrc.org.

Public Views on Same-Sex Adoption Vary

Whether gays and lesbians should be allowed to adopt children is a controversial issue. Those who are in favor of it say that children raised by homosexual parents or same-sex couples develop normally and thrive just as children with heterosexual parents. The public's views on this issue are mixed, and two polls conducted in 2007 show different results, as these charts show.

"Should gay and lesbian couples have the legal right to adopt children?"

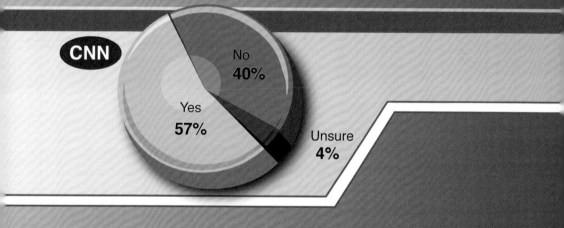

CNN

No
40%

Yes
57%

Unsure
4%

"Do you think that homosexual couples should be legally permitted to adopt children?"

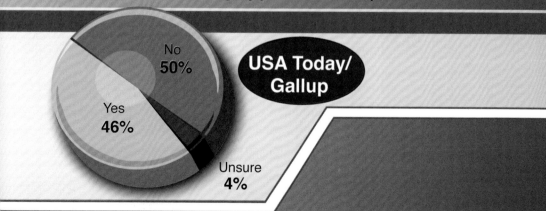

USA Today/
Gallup

No
50%

Yes
46%

Unsure
4%

*Totals could be plus or minus 3 percentage points due to sampling errors

Sources: CNN.com, "Poll Majority: Gays' Orientation Can't Change," June 27, 2007. www.cnn.com; PollingReport.com, "Law and Civil Rights," USA Today/Gallup Poll, September 7–8, 2007. www.pollingreport.com.

Same-Sex Families Have Higher Income and Education

According to a joint report by the Williams Institute and Urban Institute, same-sex parents with adopted children have higher levels of education and higher average annual household incomes than heterosexual parents.

Demographic characteristics of adoptive parents by living arrangement

	All	Same-sex couple	Different-sex married	Different-sex unmarried	Single	Same-sex female	Same-sex male
Age (average)	41.6	42.8	41.8	34.0	42.8	43.2	41.3
Education							
<High School	14%	13%	12%	28%	21%	10%	22%
High School Diploma	24%	11%	23%	36%	25%	10%	13%
Some College	32%	22%	32%	29%	32%	20%	30%
College Degree	18%	20%	19%	5%	12%	21%	16%
Graduate Studies	13%	34%	13%	2%	9%	38%	19%
Household Income	$73,274	$102,474	$81,900	$43,746	$36,312	$102,508	$102,331

Source: Gary J. Gates et al., "Adoption and Foster Care by Gay and Lesbian Parents in the United States," March 2007. www.urban.org.

- Gays and lesbians are more likely to **adopt foreign-born children** than children of American descent.

- According to the National Longitudinal Study of Adolescent Health, which surveyed **12,000 high school students**, outcomes for kids raised by homosexual parents are **comparable** to those of kids raised by heterosexual parents.

- Surveys have shown that about **45 percent** of same-sex parents are either black or Latino.

- Mississippi bans **"same-gender" couples** from adopting children, and Utah bans **adoption or fostering** by all unmarried couples, including those who are gay or lesbian.

- An October 2007 survey by the University of Arkansas showed that the **majority of respondents supported passage of the Unmarried Couple Adoption ban**, which would prohibit same-sex couples, as well as unmarried heterosexual couples, from being adoptive or foster parents.

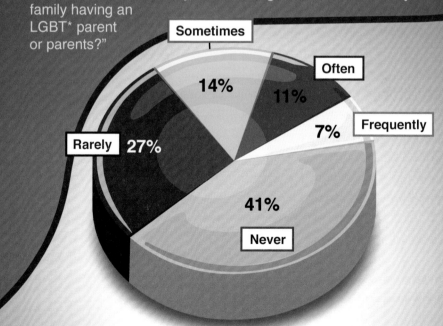

Children of Same-Sex Parents Endure Some Negative Reaction

Children who are raised by gay and lesbian parents have been the target of negative remarks about their nontraditional families by classmates. This chart shows how students responded when asked, "How often have you heard negative remarks about your family having an LGBT* parent or parents?"

Sometimes 14%
Often 11%
Frequently 7%
Rarely 27%
Never 41%

*Note: LGBT = lesbian, gay, bisexual, or transgender

What Is the Future of Gay Rights?

66 **Complete acceptance of the gay community looms somewhere in the horizon, but we can get there sooner if we demand fairness.**99

—Justin Fritscher, "It's Time to Push for Equality in Gay Rights."

66 **Homosexuality is disgusting, nauseating, shameful, wicked and vile.**99

—Iris Robinson, quoted in *New Scientist*, "Editorial: Why Homosexuality Is Not Unnatural."

The gay rights movement has come a long way since the 1960s, when gays and lesbians could not even gather in a public place without risking arrest. In many areas they live openly and do not feel the need to keep their sexual orientation a secret. Some states allow gays and lesbians to marry or form civil unions, and in almost all states they can adopt children or become foster parents. Still, however, gays and lesbians are not afforded the same federal rights as heterosexuals. They also regularly face discrimination. One example of this occurred in May 2008 during a baseball game between the Seattle Mariners and Boston Red Sox. Two lesbians who attended the game were kissing in the stands, and an usher asked them to stop, saying that their behavior was inappropriate. He told the women that a nearby fan had complained because children were in the crowd and parents would be forced to explain why two women were kissing. The incident sparked a controversy that made national headlines. Josh Friedes of Equal Rights Washington shares his views: "Certain individuals have not yet caught up. Those people see a gay or lesbian couple and they stare or say something. This is one of the challenges of being gay. Everyday things can become sources of trauma."[44]

Important Milestones

Even though gays and lesbians have not yet achieved total equality, the gay rights movement has continued to make progress over the years. One of the most important triumphs was in 2003, when in the case called *Lawrence et al. v. Texas* the Supreme Court ruled that sodomy laws in the United States were unconstitutional. The justices stated: "The liberty protected by the Constitution allows homosexual persons the right to choose to enter upon relationships in the confines of their homes and their own private lives and still retain their dignity as free person." Also included in the ruling were references to the 1986 *Bowers v. Hardwick* case, which upheld sodomy laws. The Court denounced this previous ruling by saying: "*Bowers* was not correct when it was decided, is not correct today, and is hereby overruled."[45] The ruling was considered a significant victory for gay rights because it showed that the highest court in the country could be persuaded to change its stance on an issue and even admit that it had been wrong.

Another major victory for gay rights also occurred in 2003, when the supreme court of Massachusetts declared that gays and lesbians had the right to legally marry. In the 50-page ruling, Chief Justice Margaret Marshall wrote: "We declare that barring an individual from the protections, benefits and obligations of civil marriage solely because that person would marry a person of the same sex violates the Massachusetts constitution." Marshall went on to say that the state constitution "forbids the creation of second-class citizens" and that the state attorney general, who argued that state law did not allow gays and lesbians to marry, failed to identify any constitutionally adequate reason for denying civil marriage to same-sex couples."[46] In 2008 California became the

> " The gay rights movement has come a long way since the 1960s, when gays and lesbians could not even gather in a public place without risking arrest. "

second state to legalize marriage between gay couples. Although George W. Bush has tried on several occasions to nullify these decisions with a constitutional ban on same-sex marriage, he has thus far been unsuccessful at getting such a ban passed by Congress.

> **The ruling was considered a significant victory for gay rights because it showed that the highest court in the country could be persuaded to change its stance on an issue and even admit that it had been wrong.**

In addition to growing support for gays and lesbians having the right to marry, progress has also been made in putting an end to workplace discrimination. Although many states have laws in place that protect employees from discrimination based on their sexual orientation, no federal law offers such protection. In November 2007 the U.S. House of Representatives voted in favor of the Employment Non-Discrimination Act (ENDA), which would prohibit businesses with 15 or more employees from firing, refusing to hire, or failing to promote gay or lesbian employees. To date, the Senate has not approved its own version of the bill; if it does, White House advisers said they would recommend that Bush veto it. After this was announced, the *New York Times* ran an editorial showing its support for ENDA and its strong objection to a potential veto: "Throughout American history, civil rights have been achieved in incremental steps," the editorial stated.

> The landmark Civil Rights Act of 1964, for example, barred race discrimination in public accommodations, an enormous step forward at the time. It wasn't until the next year that Congress protected voting rights in a separate bill. . . . The reasons the White House has given for opposing [ENDA]—that it would be too burdensome on businesses and that it would lead to too much litigation—echo the ones given by opponents of every previous civil rights bill to pass Congress in the past 50 years or so. That

parallel should make Mr. Bush and other opponents re-consider whether they want to be on the side of bigotry, and on the wrong side of history.[47]

A More Gay-Friendly Military?

One of the main priorities for gay and lesbian activists and advocacy groups is getting the Don't Ask, Don't Tell policy repealed. In the years since it has been in effect, thousands of military personnel have continued to be discharged solely because of their sexual orientation, which has con-tributed to a serious shortage of military personnel. Former Joint Chiefs of Staff chairman John M. Shalikashvili says that the military is "stretched thin" because of deployments in the Middle East, and all Americans who are willing and able to serve should be welcomed. He has interviewed numerous gay and lesbian military personnel and is convinced that they are now fully accepted by their peers regardless of their sexual orientation. He also cites a Zogby poll of more than 500 service members who re-turned from Afghanistan and Iraq, three-fourths of whom said that they were comfortable serving alongside gays and lesbians. For these reasons, he believes that Don't Ask, Don't Tell should be reconsidered. "By tak-ing a measured, prudent approach to change," he writes, "political and military leaders can focus on solving the nation's most pressing problems while remaining genuinely open to the eventual and inevitable lifting of the ban. When that day comes, gay men and lesbians will no longer have to conceal who they are, and the military will no longer need to sacrifice those whose service it cannot af-ford to lose."[48]

> In the years since [Don't Ask, Don't Tell] has been in effect, thousands of military personnel have continued to be discharged sole-ly because of their sexual orientation, which has contrib-uted to a serious shortage of mili-tary personnel.

The General/Flag Officers' Study Group, which is composed of re-tired officers from the Marine Corps, Air Force, and Navy, agrees that

Don't Ask, Don't Tell has outlived its usefulness. In July 2008 the group released a study that analyzed gays and lesbians in the military. Among the findings are that Don't Ask, Don't Tell policy has compelled some gays and lesbians to lie about their sexual orientation in fear of being discharged, makes it more difficult for them to perform their duties, and has prevented some from obtaining psychological and medical care and religious counseling. The report also states that the policy causes the military to lose talented service members and that allowing gays and lesbians to serve openly "is unlikely to pose any significant risk to morale, good order, discipline, or cohesion."[49] Another finding is that officers are often forced to choose between breaking the law and preserving the cohesion of their units. One heterosexual officer interviewed by the group said he suspected that one of his best troops was a lesbian. If he had been presented with credible evidence that she was, in fact, a homosexual, he said he would have chosen to break the law rather than lose someone who was so talented and valuable to his unit. The conclusion of the report is that Congress should repeal the Don't Ask, Don't Tell policy as it is no longer necessary or effective for military operations.

> " For gays and lesbians, the day when they can finally enjoy all the same rights as heterosexuals cannot possibly arrive soon enough. "

Can Homosexuality Be "Cured"?

In 1973 when the American Psychiatric Association dropped homosexuality from its list of mental disorders, gays and lesbians considered that to be a great victory. Gay rights activists had petitioned the organization for years in an effort to get the change made, using the argument that homosexuality, like race or national origin, is inborn and cannot be altered. Finally, their efforts had paid off. But Charles Socarides, a psychiatrist who led the opposition against the change, was very unhappy. His belief was that homosexuality was an illness whose effects could be reversed; through therapy, he was convinced, people could change, becoming "ex-gays" or "ex-lesbians." He often counseled gays and lesbians in his psychiatric practice, and he claimed that about 35 percent of them had "recovered" and gone on to become heterosexuals. In 1992 Socarides founded the National Association for Research & Therapy of Homosexuality (NARTH), which is dedicated to the treatment and prevention of homosexuality. NARTH's theory is that many gays and lesbians are desperately unhappy and want to change, which occurs through a process known as reparative therapy. The organization agrees with the American Psychological Association that biological, psychological, and social factors shape sexual identity at an early age for most people. NARTH, however, places the most emphasis on psychological factors such as family, peer groups, and social influences. Its members, many of whom refer to themselves as "recovered" gays or lesbians, denounce the belief that homosexuality is purely biological. As NARTH's Web site states:

> There is no such thing as a "gay gene" and there is no evidence to support the idea that homosexuality is simply genetic. However, biological influences may indeed influence some people toward homosexuality; recent studies point to prenatal-hormonal influences, especially in men, that result in a low-masculinized brain; also, there may be genetic factors in some people—both of which would affect gender identity, and therefore sexual orientation. But none of these factors mean that homosexuality is normal and a part of human design, or that it is inevitable in such people, or that it is unchangeable. Numerous examples exist of people who have successfully modified their sexual behavior, identity, and arousal or fantasies.[50]

NARTH is a highly controversial organization. Many psychologists, psychiatrists, and other mental health professionals denounce reparative therapy, saying that it can be harmful and even dangerous for gays and lesbians. Psychotherapist Gary Greenberg explains:

> All the major psychotherapy guilds have barred their members from researching or practicing reparative therapy on the grounds that it is inherently unethical to treat something that is not a disease, that it contributes to

oppression by pathologizing homosexuality, and that it is dangerous to patients whose self-esteem can only suffer when they try to change something about themselves that they can't (and shouldn't have to) change.[51]

What Tomorrow Holds

The gay rights movement has progressed slowly over the years, but it has achieved a number of important victories. Sodomy laws have been unconstitutional since 2003 and in a number of states gays and lesbians can no longer be discriminated against in the workplace, in housing, or in public accommodations. Homosexual marriages are legal in two states, and in several others gays and lesbians may form civil unions that afford most or all of the same rights that are granted to married heterosexuals. A proposed constitutional ban on gay marriage has been struck down twice by Congress, and a first step has been taken toward federal antidiscriminatory workplace legislation. Strong, powerful gay rights organizations such as the ACLU, the Gay Liberation Front, and the National Gay and Lesbian Task Force, constantly advocate for gays and lesbians, helping them fight for their rights. Much progress has been made over the years—yet even now, gays and lesbians still face many hurdles, such as the military's Don't Ask, Don't Tell policy and the ban on same-sex marriages in a majority of states, as well as outright hatred by those who angrily declare that gays and lesbians are living in sin. As time goes by, public attitudes will likely become more accepting, as the attitudes today are certainly much different from those of the 1950s and 1960s when being homosexual meant living in secret and in fear. For gays and lesbians, the day when they can finally enjoy all the same rights as heterosexuals cannot possibly arrive soon enough.

Primary Source Quotes*

What Is the Future of Gay Rights?

❝I am almost 72, and I have been hated all my life, and I don't see much change coming. I think your hate is evil.❞

—Larry Kramer, "Why Do Straights Hate Gays?" *Los Angeles Times*, March 20, 2007. www.latimes.com.

Kramer is the founder of the advocacy and protest organization AIDS Coalition to Unleash Power (ACT UP) and cofounder of the Gay Men's Health Crisis, the world's largest provider of services to those with AIDS.

❝The homosexual agenda is destroying this nation. . . . I honestly think it's the biggest threat that our nation has, even more so than terrorism or Islam.❞

—Sally Kern, quoted in Fox News, "Oklahoma Rep. Sally Kern on YouTube Clip: Homosexuality Bigger Threat than Terrorism," March 16, 2008. www.foxnews.com.

Kern is a state representative from Oklahoma City.

* Editor's Note: While the definition of a primary source can be narrowly or broadly defined, for the purposes of Compact Research, a primary source consists of: 1) results of original research presented by an organization or researcher; 2) eyewitness accounts of events, personal experience, or work experience; 3) first-person editorials offering pundits' opinions; 4) government officials presenting political plans and/or policies; 5) representatives of organizations presenting testimony or policy.

Primary Source Quotes

❝Watching the growing conflict between medical science and religion over homosexuality is like watching a train wreck from a distance. You can see it coming for miles and sense the inevitable conclusion, but you're powerless to stop it. The more church leaders dig in their heels, the worse it's likely to be.❞

—Oliver "Buzz" Thomas, "When Religion Loses Its Credibility," *USA Today*, November 19, 2006. www.usatoday.com.

Thomas is a Baptist minister and author of the book *10 Things Your Minister Wants to Tell You (but Can't Because He Needs the Job)*.

❝An honest reading of Scripture will always lead one to acknowledge that homosexuality is a sin and is condemned by God.❞

—Reverend Dale Lee, "What the Bible Says About Homosexuality," *Watchmen on the Wall*, Family Research Council, May 31, 2007. www.frc.org.

Lee is the Family Research Council's special assistant to the president for pastoral ministries.

❝Many myopic, delusional individuals still believe that homosexuality is a disease relegated to the fringes of society. . . . It is an immutable genetic trait and not a 'choice' as some demagogues have preached to a conformist, and at times ignorant, public.❞

—Rena Ganz, "Mainstreaming Gay Marriage," *Knight News*, November 11, 2007. www.qcknightnews.com.

Ganz is a columnist for the *Knight News*.

66 Despite ongoing efforts, researchers have not discovered a biological basis for same-sex attractions.99

—Julie Harren, "Homosexuality 101: What Every Therapist, Parent, and Homosexual Should Know,"
National Association for Research & Therapy of Homosexuality (NARTH), April 9, 2008.

Harren is an assistant professor of psychology at Palm Beach Atlantic University, as well as a licensed marriage and family therapist.

....

66 And do not tell me you are 'tolerant' or 'tolerate' gay people. Stop for a moment and think about how condescending and evil that attitude is.99

—Michael S. Miller, "Gay Rights and Wrongs," *Toledo Free Press*, April 4, 2008. www.toledofreepress.com.

Miller is editor in chief of the *Toledo Free Press*.

....

66 In 2008, denying gay Americans the opportunity to marry is not only inhumane, it is unsustainable. History has turned a corner: Gay couples—including gay parents—live openly and for the most part comfortably in mainstream life. This will not change, ever.99

—Jonathan Rauch, "Gay Marriage Is Good for America," *Wall Street Journal*, June 21, 2008. www.wsj.com.

Rauch is a senior writer with *National Journal* and a guest scholar at the Brookings Institution.

....

❝Until recently, growing up gay meant awaiting a lifetime of secrecy—furtive encounters, darkened bar windows, crushing deracination. That has changed with shocking speed.❞

—John Cloud, "The Battle over Gay Teens," *Time,* October 2, 2005. www.time.com.

Cloud is a staff writer for *Time* magazine.

....

❝Mark these words, my friends—there'll come a time when same-sex marriages will be as commonplace as people of different skin tone eating in the same restaurant. Then, as now, we will look on a time when people were discriminated against and we'll ask, 'What the hell were people thinking back then?'❞

—D. Allan Kerr, "Prediction: Gay Marriage Will Be Protected Under Constitution," Seacoastonline, June 1, 2008. www.seacoastonline.com.

Kerr is a novelist and former newspaper reporter.

....

Facts and Illustrations

What Is the Future of Gay Rights?

- The gay rights movement's two top priorities are **repealing the military's Don't Ask, Don't Tell policy** and achieving the legal right for same-sex couples to marry in any state.

- A 2008 report by the General/Flag Officers' Study Group shows that the **Don't Ask, Don't Tell** policy is no longer needed and should be repealed.

- In a Zogby poll of more than **500 military service members** who returned from Afghanistan and Iraq, **75 percent** of respondents said that they were comfortable serving alongside gays and lesbians.

- In 2005 the technology giant **Microsoft** announced that it would publicly support initiatives that protected the rights of gays and lesbians in the workplace.

- In November 2007 the U.S. House of Representatives voted in favor of the **Employment Non-Discrimination Act** (ENDA), which would prohibit businesses with 15 or more employees from firing, refusing to hire, or failing to promote gay or lesbian employees. The bill has yet to pass in the Senate.

- In 2007 the U.S. House and Senate voted to add **"sexual orientation"** to **hate crimes** legislation.

Seeking Equality in the Military

One of the primary goals of the gay rights movement is getting the Don't Ask, Don't Tell policy repealed. Many military personnel, including officers and retired officers, believe that the policy is no longer needed and, in fact, causes more harm than it does good. An opinion poll conducted by Zogby International in October 2006, which involved 545 members of the armed services, found that most respondents had little or no aversion toward gays and lesbians serving in the military.

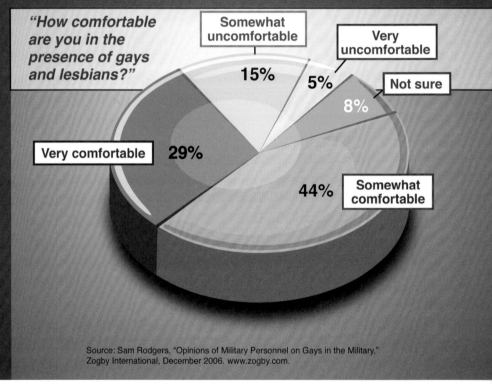

"How comfortable are you in the presence of gays and lesbians?"

Somewhat uncomfortable 15%

Very uncomfortable 5%

Not sure 8%

Very comfortable 29%

Somewhat comfortable 44%

Source: Sam Rodgers, "Opinions of Military Personnel on Gays in the Military," Zogby International, December 2006. www.zogby.com.

- As of July 2008 several hundred municipalities and **20 states had approved bans** on employment discrimination based on sexual orientation.

- After a fight that lasted nearly 30 years, the state of Washington approved the **revision of a law banning discrimination** in housing, employment, and insurance to include "sexual orientation."

Gay Rights Progress

Even though gays and lesbians are still not afforded all the same rights as heterosexuals, the gay rights movement has achieved some major victories throughout the years, as this chart shows.

1960	2008
Sodomy laws in all states criminalize homosexual acts between consenting adults	Sodomy laws technically exist but have been ruled unconstitutional by the Supreme Court
Homosexuality considered a mental illness	The American Psychiatric Association no longer lists homosexuality as a mental illness, and denounces bias based on sexual orientation
U.S. Department of Defense bans gays and lesbians from serving in the military	Gays and lesbians may serve in the military if they keep their sexual orientation a secret
Employees of the federal government may be denied employment, fired from their jobs, or be kept from promotions based on sexual orientation	Gay and lesbian federal employees are protected from workplace discrimination
The McCarra-Walters Act bans "sexual deviates" from immigrating to the United States, which the U.S. Supreme Court says applies to gays and lesbians	McCarra-Walters Act no longer in force; ruled unconstitutional
U.S. Department of Justice neither collects nor reports statistics on hate crimes that involve homosexuals	Department of Justice collects and records statistics on hate crimes that involve homosexuals
Gay marriage is illegal in all states	Gay marriage is legal in California and Massachusetts, and seven states and the District of Columbia allow various types of legal unions
Gay and lesbians prohibited from adopting children	Gays and lesbians, either as singles or same-sex couples, may adopt children in 49 U.S. states

Sources: Public Agenda, "A History of Gay and Lesbian Rights," 2007. www.publicagenda.org; Dudley Clendiner, "Gay Rights Movement in the United States," Microsoft Encarta, 2008. http://encarta.msn-ppe.com.

Sexual Orientation Hate Crime Legislation

Although the U.S. House of Representatives voted in 2007 to expand existing hate crime legislation so it includes sexual orientation, there is currently no federal law that specifically protects gays and lesbians from being victimized by hate crimes. However, some states have their own laws in place.

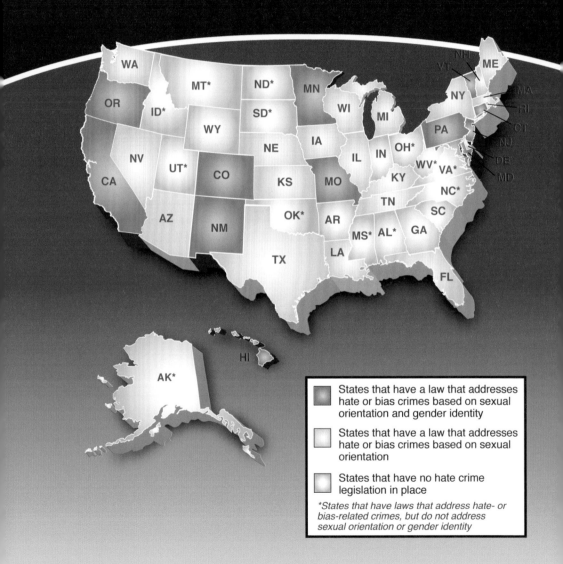

States that have a law that addresses hate or bias crimes based on sexual orientation and gender identity

States that have a law that addresses hate or bias crimes based on sexual orientation

States that have no hate crime legislation in place

*States that have laws that address hate- or bias-related crimes, but do not address sexual orientation or gender identity

Source: Human Rights Campaign Foundation, "State Hate Crimes Laws," January 23, 2008. www.hrc.org.

- In October 2007 **antihomosexual activists** in Oregon failed to get enough signatures to ban the Oregon Equality Act.

- A September 2008 survey of Florida voters showed that **55 percent** supported a constitutional amendment that would define marriage as a legal union between a man and a woman, thus making same-sex marriage illegal in the state, down from **58 percent** in a June 2008 survey.

- A May 2008 "Values and Beliefs" poll by Gallup showed that **48 percent** of respondents believed homosexual relations was morally acceptable, and **48 percent** said it was morally wrong.

- According to Harris Interactive's "2008 Out & Equal Workplace Survey," **79 percent** of heterosexual adults agree that how someone does on the job should be the standard for judging an employee, not his or her sexual orientation, which is a slight increase from **77 percent** in 2002.

Key People and Advocacy Groups

American Civil Liberties Union (ACLU): An advocacy group whose mission is to preserve the protections and guarantees afforded to *all* Americans through the U.S. Constitution.

J. Matt Barber: A strong, vocal opponent of homosexuality who is adamantly against same-sex marriage and the ability of gays and lesbians to adopt children.

Anita Bryant: A former beauty queen and pop singer from Miami who became an outspoken activist against homosexuality, Bryant spearheaded a movement called "Save Our Children from Homosexuals."

James C. Dobson: The founder of the Christian organization Focus on the Family.

Jerry Falwell: Before his death in 2007, Falwell was a fundamentalist Baptist minister from Lynchberg, Virginia. He founded the group called the Moral Majority.

Gay Liberation Front: A gay and lesbian activist group founded in 1969 after the Stonewall Riots.

Henry Gerber: The founder of the Society for Human Rights, the first group in the United States to advocate for civil rights for homosexuals.

Barbara Gittings: A lesbian woman who founded the New York City chapter of the activist group Daughters of Bilitis.

Harry Hay: An American Communist who founded the homosexual advocacy group Mattachine Society in Los Angeles in 1950.

Larry Kramer: A playwright, screenwriter, and gay rights activist who founded the protest organization known as AIDS Coalition to Unleash

Power (ACT UP), and who cofounded the Gay Men's Health Crisis, the world's largest provider of services to those with AIDS.

Del Martin and Phyllis Lyon: Gay rights activists and partners for more than 50 years, Martin and Lyon were the first to be married in June 2008 after the California Supreme Court struck down a law that forbade same-sex marriages.

Harvey Milk: A well-known San Francisco politician and gay rights activist who was gunned down and killed in 1978 by a former police officer. Milk's death sparked a gay rights revolution and annual marches in Washington, D.C.

Gavin Newsom: As the mayor of San Francisco, Newsom gained national attention in 2004 when he directed county officials to issue marriage licenses to same-sex couples. The California Supreme Court struck down the ruling four years later.

Elaine Noble: A speech professor at Boston's Emerson College who in 1974 became the first openly homosexual candidate to be elected to state office in the United States.

Chronology

1951
Writing under an assumed name, "Donald Webster Cory" releases *The Homosexual in America*, the first book written by a gay man on what life is like for homosexuals.

1924
The Society for Human Rights, the first group in the United States to advocate for civil rights for homosexuals, is founded in Chicago by Henry Gerber.

1950
The Mattachine Society, a secretive network of homosexuals, is founded in Los Angeles by American Communist Harry Hay.

1974
Elaine Noble, a speech professor at Boston's Emerson College, becomes the first openly homosexual candidate to be elected to state office in the United States.

1948
The first survey of America's sex habits, *Sexual Behavior in the Human Male*, is published by zoologist Alfred Kinsey.

1965
A small group of gay men and lesbians hold a demonstration in front of the Liberty Bell in Philadelphia, during which they protest discrimination against gays and lesbians.

1930 1940 1950 1960 1970

1953
President Dwight D. Eisenhower issues an executive order that bars homosexual men and women from holding any federal jobs.

1969
After a popular gay bar in New York City's Greenwich Village is raided by police, the streets erupt in a violent protest involving thousands of people. It later becomes known as the Stonewall Riots.

1955
Eight lesbian women, including activists/partners Del Martin and Phyllis Lyon, found the Daughters of Bilitis, a social group in San Francisco that becomes a powerful force in the gay rights movement.

1973
After years of declaring homosexuality to be a mental illness, the American Psychiatric Association (APA) declares that homosexuals are not insane and votes 13 to 0 to remove homosexuality from its *DSM-II*, the official manual of psychiatric disorders. The APA also denounces discrimination against gays and lesbians and calls for them to receive the same protections guaranteed to other citizens.

1978
Harvey Milk, a well-known San Francisco politician and gay rights activist, is gunned down and killed by a former police officer.

1981
The U.S. Department of Defense adopts a ban on gays and lesbians in the military.

1984
The cause of AIDS, which is claiming lives at a frightful rate of speed, is announced to be the human immunodeficiency virus (HIV).

1987
The international advocacy and protest organization known as AIDS Coalition to Unleash Power (ACT UP) is founded in New York City by gay rights activist and screenwriter Larry Kramer.

1995
President Bill Clinton ends the ban on national security clearances for gays and lesbians.

2007
A proposed constitutional ban on same-sex marriage is defeated by a joint session of the U.S. Legislature, eliminating any chance of getting it on the ballot for the November 2008 election.

2000
Vermont becomes the first state to allow civil unions between same-sex partners, giving them most of the benefits of marriage.

2004
Massachusetts becomes the first state to legalize marriage between same-sex partners.

1985   **1990**   **1995**   **2000**   **2005**

1993
The U.S. Congress passes the Don't Ask, Don't Tell policy, which holds that gays and lesbians are still not officially allowed to serve in the military, but they will be tolerated as long as they do not make their sexual orientation known and do not act on it.

1998
Clinton issues an executive order prohibiting discrimination based on sexual orientation in most federal civilian hiring.

2008
The California Supreme Court declares the state's ban on same-sex marriage to be unconstitutional.

1986
The U.S. Supreme Court upholds an 1816 Georgia sodomy law, declaring that states have the right to prosecute homosexual relations as a felony.

1996
Clinton signs legislation known as the Defense of Marriage Act, which defines marriage as a union between a man and a woman.

1983
Reverend Jerry Falwell publically calls AIDS the "gay plague."

2003
In a case known as *Lawrence et al. v. Texas*, the U.S. Supreme Court rules that sodomy laws in the United States are unconstitutional, and adults have the right to engage in private conduct without government interference.

Related Organizations

American Civil Liberties Union (ACLU)

125 Broad St., 18th Floor

New York, NY 10004

phone: (212) 549-2627

e-mail: info@aclu.org

Web site: www.aclu.org

The ACLU's mission is to preserve the protections and guarantees afforded to Americans through the U.S. Constitution. Its Lesbian Gay Bisexual Transgender (LGBT) Project is devoted to fighting discrimination and influencing public opinion on LGBT rights through the courts, legislatures, and public education. Its Web site offers numerous fact sheets, research publications, news stories, legislative updates, and a wide variety of other resources.

Campaign for Children and Families (CCF)

PO Box 511

Sacramento, CA 95812

phone: (916) 265-5650

fax: (916) 848-3456

Web site: www.saveamerica.net

CCF stands for traditional family values, male/female marriage, parental rights, and the sanctity of human life. Its Web site features numerous articles, news releases, media interviews, and a "Get Informed" section with bulletins, current issues, and a link to broadcasts of the U.S. Congress and California legislative meetings.

Children of Lesbians and Gays Everywhere (COLAGE)

1550 Bryant St., Suite 830

San Francisco, CA 94103

phone: (415) 861-5437

fax: (415) 255-8345

e-mail: info@colage.org

Web site: www.colage.org

COLAGE is a national movement of children, youth, and adults with one or more lesbian, gay, bisexual, and/or transgender parents. The organization seeks to work toward social justice through youth empowerment, leadership development, education, and advocacy. Its Web site offers various publications, research papers, a pen pal program, a "Creative Corner" section, and a newsletter entitled *Just for Us*.

Coalition for Positive Sexuality (CPS)

PO Box 77212

Washington, DC 20013-7212

phone: (773) 604-1654

Web site: www.positive.org

The CPS is an activist organization that is dedicated to providing teens with candid, informative sex education materials. Its Web site features a bulletin board called "Let's Talk," a state-by-state listing of parental consent laws, and a list of Internet resources of interest to young people.

Family Equality Council

PO Box 206

Boston, MA 02133

phone: (617) 502-8700

fax: (617) 502-8701

e-mail: info@familyequality.org

Web site: www.familyequality.org

Originally called the Gay Fathers Coalition, the Family Equality Council works to ensure equality for lesbian, gay, bisexual, and transgendered families through advocacy, education, and the promotion of positive public policy. Its Web site features a message board, numerous publications, research papers, and an "Ask the Experts" section where people can ask difficult questions.

Family Research Council (FRC)

801 G St. NW

Washington, DC 20001

phone: (202) 393-2100

fax: (202) 393-2134

Web site: www.frc.org

The FRC is an educational organization that reaffirms and promotes heterosexual marriage and traditional family values. Its Web site features expert testimonies, a wide variety of "issues" papers, press releases, and news stories.

Focus on the Family

Colorado Springs, CO 80995

phone: (719) 531-5181; toll-free: (800) 232-6459

fax: (719) 531-3424

Web site: www.fotf.org

Focus on the Family promotes traditional Christian values and strong family ties by disseminating resource information on marriage, parenting, and family life, as well as conducting research and education programs. Numerous publications are available on its Web site dealing with such issues as life challenges, social issues, marriage, parenting, and faith.

Gay and Lesbian Alliance Against Defamation (GLAAD)

5455 Wilshire Blvd., #1500

Los Angeles, CA 90036

phone: (323) 933-2240

fax: (323) 933-2241

Web site: www.glaad.org

GLAAD is a nonprofit organization dedicated to promoting and ensuring fair, accurate, and inclusive representation of people and events in the media in order to eliminate homophobia and discrimination based on gender identity and sexual orientation. Its Web site offers press releases, resource kits, news stories, and publications that cover a wide variety of topics.

Gay and Lesbian Victory Fund

1133 15th St. NW, Suite 350

Washington, DC 20005

phone: (202) 842-8679

fax: (202) 289-3863

Web site: www.victoryfund.org

The Gay and Lesbian Victory Fund is a political action committee (PAC) that is committed to increasing the number of openly gay and lesbian elected officials at all levels of government. Its Web site features information about candidates running for office, a candidate "election scorecard," news articles, and a podcast.

Gay, Lesbian, and Straight Education Network (GLSEN)

90 Broad St., 2nd Floor

New York, NY 10004

phone: (212) 727-0135

fax: (212) 727-0254

e-mail: glsen@glsen.org

Web site: www.glsen.org

GLSEN is a national organization that seeks to end discrimination based on sexual orientation in public schools. Its Web site provides news articles as well as a library of more than 1,000 resources that can be searched for by keyword and topic.

Heritage Foundation

214 Massachusetts Ave. NE

Washington, DC 20002

phone: (202) 546-4400

fax: (202) 546-8328

e-mail: info@heritage.org

Web site: www.heritage.org

The Heritage Foundation is a research and educational institute (think tank) whose mission is to develop and promote conservative public policies based on the principles of free enterprise, limited government, individual freedoms, and traditional American values. Its Web site features news articles covering a variety of topics, research papers, and a large "Issues" section.

National Gay and Lesbian Task Force

1325 Massachusetts Ave. NW, Suite 600

Washington, DC 20005

phone: (202) 393-5177

fax: (202) 393-2241

e-mail: info@thetaskforce.org

Web site: www.thetaskforce.org

The National Gay and Lesbian Task Force, which calls itself "the uncompromising national voice for full LGBT equality," works to ensure the civil rights of gay, lesbian, bisexual, and transgendered people by building a powerful political movement. Its Web site features a searchable database of numerous publications, as well as news stories, a "hate crimes law map," reports, and fact sheets.

Parents, Families, and Friends of Lesbians and Gays (PFLAG)

1726 M St. NW, Suite 400

Washington, DC 20003

phone: (202) 467-8180

fax: (202) 467-8194

e-mail: info@pflag.org

Web site: www.pflag.org

PFLAG is a national organization that promotes the health and well-being of gays and lesbians, as well as their families and friends, through support, education, and advocacy. Its Web site features policy statements, an "online newsroom" with a variety of news stories, and a special section for families and friends.

Traditional Values Coalition (TVC)

139 C St. SE

Washington, DC 20003

phone: (202) 547-8570

fax: (202) 546-6403

Web site: www.traditionalvalues.org

The TVC is a nondenominational, grassroots church lobby that emphasizes the restoration of the values needed to maintain strong, unified families. Its Web site features editorials, press releases, news stories, special reports, and "action alerts."

For Further Research

Books

Alan Chambers, ed., *God's Grace and the Homosexual Next Door*. Eugene, OR: Harvest House, 2006.

Joe Dallas, *When Homosexuality Hits Home*. Eugene, OR: Harvest House, 2004.

Steve Endean, *Bringing Lesbian and Gay Rights into the Mainstream*. New York: Harrington Park, 2006.

Fred Fejes, *Gay Rights and Moral Panic*. New York: Palgrave Macmillan, 2008.

Robert J. Gagnon and Dan O. Via, *Homosexuality and the Bible: Two Views*. Minneapolis: Fortress, 2003.

Mike Haley, *101 Frequently Asked Questions About Homosexuality*. Eugene, OR: Harvest House, 2004.

H.N. Hirsch, *The Future of Gay Rights in America*. New York: Routledge, 2005.

Lisa Keen, *Out Law: What LGBT Youth Should Know About Their Legal Rights*. Boston: Beacon, 2007.

Francis MacNutt, *Can Homosexuality Be Healed?* Grand Rapids, MI: Chosen Books, 2006.

Eric Marcus, *Making Gay History*. New York: Perennial, 2002.

David Moats, *Civil Wars: The Battle for Gay Marriage*. Orlando, FL: Harcourt, 2005.

Richard Mohr, *The Long Arc of Justice*. New York: Columbia University Press, 2007.

David A. Richards, *The Case for Gay Rights*. Lawrence: University Press of Kansas, 2005.

Craig A. Rimmerman, *The Lesbian and Gay Movements: Assimilation or Liberation*. Boulder, CO: Westview, 2008.

Brette McWhorter Sember, *Gay and Lesbian Rights*. 2nd ed. Naperville, IL: Sphinx, 2006.

Angela Watrous and Meredith Maran, *50 Ways to Support Lesbian and Gay Equality*. Maui, HI: Inner Ocean, 2005.

Evan Wolfson, *Why Marriage Matters*. New York: Simon & Schuster, 2004.

Periodicals

Ryan T. Anderson, "Beyond Gay Marriage," *The Weekly Standard*, August 15, 2006.

Deborah Baer, "The Story of My Coming Out," *CosmoGirl*, April 2008, p. 125.

Jim David, "Antigay and Proud," *Advocate*, January 29, 2008, p. 20.

Midge Decter, "Stop Compromising on 'Civil Unions,'" *USA Today Magazine*, March 2007, pp. 52–53.

Beren deMotier, "Out with My Son," *Curve*, May 2008, p. 63.

Mike Dumont, "Debate on Gays Serving Petty in Dangerous Times," *Officer*, January 2008, p. 11.

Susana T. Fried, "Two Steps Forward, One Step Back," *Conscience*, Spring 2006, pp. 23–25.

Marina Gatto, "Coming Out (When Your Parents Are Gay)," *CosmoGirl*, April 2007, p. 145.

Alastair Gee, "In Russia, Gays and Lesbians Struggle Against Widespread Hostility," *U.S. News & World Report*, May 29, 2008.

Gary Greenberg, "Gay by Choice?" *Mother Jones*, September/October 2007, pp. 60–67.

Kate Lacey, "Coming Out to Your Parents," *Curve*, October 2007, pp. 30–32.

Amy McDougall and Jake Nyberg, "Mutual Grace: Gay Rights Activists Seek—and Find—Dialogue on (Some) Christian Campuses," *Sojourners Magazine*, September/October 2006.

Bruce C. Steele, "A Tale of Two Zachs," *Advocate*, July 19, 2005, p. 6.

Laura J. Weinstock, "Love Is Not Violence," *Advocate*, July 19, 2005, p. 72.

Internet Sources

American Psychological Association, *Lesbian & Gay Parenting*, 2005. www.apa.org/pi/lgbc/publications/lgparenting.pdf.

John Cloud, "The Battle over Gay Teens," *Time*, October 2, 2005. www.time.com/time/magazine/article/0,9171,1112856,00.html.

Rena Ganz, "Mainstreaming Gay Marriage," *Knight News*, November 7, 2007. www.qcknightnews.com/media/storage/paper564/news/2007/11/07/Opinion/Mainstreaming.Gay.Marriage-3097495.shtml.

Josh Gibbs, "It's Time to Allow Gays to Serve Openly in the Military," *Marine Corps Times*, April 23, 2007. www.marinecorpstimes.com/community/opinion/marine_opinion_gibbs_070423.

Michael Glatze, "How a 'Gay Rights' Leader Became Straight," *World-Net Daily*, July 3, 2007. www.wnd.com/news/article.asp?ARTICLE_ID=56487.

Tyler Gray, "The Gay Baby," *St. Petersburg Times*, March 18, 2007. www.sptimes.com/2007/03/18/Opinion/The_gay_baby.shtml.

David Jefferson, "How AIDS Changed America," *Newsweek*, May 15, 2006. www.newsweek.com/id/47748?tid=relatedcl.

Garrison Keillor, "Stating the Obvious," *Salon*, March 14, 2007. www.salon.com/opinion/feature/2007/03/14/keillor.

Larry Kramer, "Why Do Straights Hate Gays?" *Los Angeles Times*, March 20, 2007. www.latimes.com/news/opinion/la-oe-kramer20mar20,0,1705133.story?coll=la-opinion-rightrail.

Jeninne Lee–St. John, "Viewpoint: Civil Rights and Gay Rights," *Time*, October 25, 2005. www.time.com/time/nation/article/0,8599,1121811,00.html.

Michael S. Miller, "Gay Rights and Wrongs," *Toledo Free Press*, April 4, 2008. www.toledofreepress.com/?id=7513.

Anna Quindlen, "The Same People," *Newsweek*, June 9, 2008. www.newsweek.com/id/139423.

William Saletan, "Don't Do unto Others," *Slate*, March 23, 2006. www.slate.com/id/2138482.

Scott Sherman, "If Our Son Is Happy, What Else Matters?" *Newsweek*, September 16, 2002. www.newsweek.com/id/65655.

Source Notes

Overview

1. Ken Harlin, "The Stonewall Riot and Its Aftermath," *Stonewall and Beyond: Lesbian and Gay Culture*, Columbia University, September 27, 2004. www.columbia.edu.
2. *Bowers v. Hardwick*, 478 U.S. 186 (1986). http://caselaw.lp.findlaw.com.
3. *Lawrence et al. v. Texas*, 539 U.S. 558 (2003). www.law.cornell.edu.
4. Larry Kramer, "Why Do Straights Hate Gays?" *Los Angeles Times*, March 20, 2007. www.latimes.com.
5. Quoted in Deb Price, "How Falwell Helped Foster Gay Rights Progress," *National Gay News*, May 21, 2007. http://nationalgaynews.com.
6. Hugh Aitken et al., "Report of the General/Flag Officers' Study Group," 2008. www.palmcenter.org.
7. Josh Gibbs, "It's Time to Allow Gays to Serve Openly in the Military," *Marine Corps Times*, April 23, 2007. www.marinecorpstimes.com.
8. Gibbs, "It's Time to Allow Gays to Serve Openly in the Military."
9. Quoted in Mackenzie Carpenter, "What Happens to Kids Raised by Gay Parents?" *Pittsburgh Post-Gazette*, June 10, 2007. www.post-gazette.com.
10. Quoted in Rachanee Srisavasdi, "City to Pay Gay Officer Up to $2.15 Million," *Orange County Register*, June 30, 2008. www.ocregister.com.
11. James C. Dobson, "Two Mommies Is One Too Many," *Time*, December 12, 2006. www.time.com.
12. Quoted in Carpenter, "What Happens to Kids Raised by Gay Parents?"
13. Gibbs, "It's Time to Allow Gays to Serve Openly in the Military."

Are Gay Rights Protected in the United States?

14. Quoted in Duane Wells, "Hypocrite of the Week: Oregon State Senator, Gary George," GayWired, March 21, 2008. www.gaywired.com.
15. Quoted in Ann Rostow, "Boy Says Mom Is Gay; School Rebukes Him," Gay.com, December 1, 2003. www.gay.com.
16. Quoted in Rostow, "Boy Says Mom Is Gay."
17. Quoted in Rostow, "Boy Says Mom Is Gay."
18. Quoted in Rostow, "Boy Says Mom Is Gay."
19. Quoted in American Civil Liberties Union, "ACLU Gives Tennessee High School an F in Civics for Censoring Gay and Gay-Supportive Students," May 14, 2007. www.aclu.org.
20. American Civil Liberties Union, "Appeals Court Rules in Favor of Decorated Air Force Major Discharged on Grounds of Sexual Orientation," May 21, 2008. www.aclu.org.
21. Quoted in American Civil Liberties Union, "Appeals Court Rules in Favor of Decorated Air Force Major Discharged on Grounds of Sexual Orientation."
22. Quoted in ABC News, "New Details Emerge in Matthew Shepard Murder," November 26, 2004. http://abcnews.go.com.
23. Robert Knight, "'Hate Crimes' Bill: Prescription for Tyranny," *WorldNet Daily*, May 29, 2004. www.worldnetdaily.com.
24. Jennifer Vanasco, "Let Liberty Ring!" Independent Gay Forum, July 13, 2008. www.indegayforum.org.

Should Gays and Lesbians Have the Legal Right to Marry?

25. Quoted in Jesse McKinley, "Gay Couples Rejoice at Ruling," *New York Times*, May 16, 2008. www.nytimes.com.

26. Quoted in Sarah Varney, "Octogenarian Gay-Rights Pioneers Wed in California," National Public Radio, June 17, 2008. www.npr.org.

27. League of Women Voters, "Proposition 22: Limit on Marriages," April 13, 2000. www.smartvoter.org.

28. J. Matt Barber, "Children in the 'Gay Marriage' Crosshairs," *Culture and Family Issues*, Concerned Women for America (CWA), July 3, 2008. www.cwfa.org.

29. Carol A. Corrigan, "Concurring and Dissenting Opinion by Corrigan, J.," Supreme Court of California, in re Marriage Cases, May 15, 2008. www.courtinfo.ca.gov.

30. Kevin McCullough, "Why Homosexuals Despise Marriage," *WorldNet Daily*, October 22, 2006. www.wnd.com.

31. George W. Bush, "President Calls for Constitutional Amendment Protecting Marriage," *Remarks by the President*, news release, White House, February 24, 2004. www.whitehouse.gov.

Should Gays and Lesbians Raise Children?

32. Scott Sherman, "If Our Son Is Happy, What Else Matters?" *Newsweek*, September 16, 2002. www.newsweek.com.

33. Sherman, "If Our Son Is Happy, What Else Matters?"

34. *American Heritage Dictionary*, 2006. http://dictionary.reference.com.

35. Glenn T. Stanton, "Is Marriage in Jeopardy?" Focus on the Family. www.family.org.

36. American Psychological Association, *Lesbian & Gay Parenting*, 2005. www.apa.org.

37. Moriah Ford-Gowan, "Gay Parents," letter to the editor, *National Catholic Reporter*, February 2, 2007, p. 20.

38. Ford-Gowan, "Gay Parents."

39. Quoted in Carpenter, "What Happens to Kids Raised by Gay Parents?"

40. Quoted in Carpenter, "What Happens to Kids Raised by Gay Parents?"

41. Robin Sclafani, "Experiences of Children with Gay Parents," *ILGA-Europe Newsletter*, Spring 2006. www.ceji.org.

42. Dahlia Lithwick, "Why Courts Are Adopting Gay Parenting," *Washington Post*, March 12, 2006. www.washingtonpost.com.

43. Jennifer Chrisler, "Two Mommies or Two Daddies Will Do Fine, Thanks," *Time*, December 14, 2006. www.time.com.

What Is the Future of Gay Rights?

44. Quoted in Fox News, "Lesbian Kiss Sparks Controversy at Seattle Mariners' Ballpark," June 5, 2008. www.foxnews.com.

45. *Lawrence et al. v. Texas*.

46. Quoted in Kathleen Burge, "SJC: Gay Marriage Legal in Mass.," *Boston Globe*, November 18, 2003. www.boston.com

47. *New York Times*, "An Overdue Step for Equal Justice," November 9, 2007. www.nytimes.com.

48. John M. Shalikashvili, "Second Thoughts on Gays in the Military," *New York Times*, January 2, 2007. www.nytimes.com.

49. Aitken et al., "Report of the General/Flag Officers' Study Group."

50. National Association for Research & Therapy of Homosexuality (NARTH), "Position Statement: On the Causes of Homosexuality," February 28, 2008. www.narth.com.

51. Gary Greenberg, "Gay by Choice?" *Mother Jones*, September/October 2007, p. 61.

List of Illustrations

Index

About the Author

Peggy J. Parks holds a bachelor of science degree from Aquinas College in Grand Rapids, Michigan, where she graduated magna cum laude. She is an author who has written more than 70 nonfiction educational books for children and young adults, as well as self-published her own cookbook called *Welcome Home: Recipes, Memories, and Traditions from the Heart.* Parks lives in Muskegon, Michigan, a town that she says inspires her writing because of its location on the shores of Lake Michigan.